MONEY~MAKING
IDEAS
FOR RETIREES

D1457987

By Ronald J. Cooke

Longman Financial Services Publishing
a division of Longman Financial Services Institute, Inc.

First published in 1983 by Stoddart Publishing.
Reprinted 1985. Reprinted in 1989 by
Longman Financial Services Publishing, a division
of Longman Financial Services Institute, Inc.

ISBN 0-88462-879-5

Canadian Cataloguing in Publication Data
Cooke, Ronald J., 1913-
    Money-making ideas for retirees
ISBN 0-7737-5023-1
1. Retirement income. 2. Self-employed. 1. Title
HQ1062.C66   646.7'9   C83-098032-6

Printed and bound in Canada

CONTENTS

6

Dedicated to senior citizens
everywhere, without whom
this world would
indeed be a dismal place.

FOREWORD

It All Began Over One Hundred Years Ago

*I*t was in Germany that sixty-five year olds first became recognized as an important group of people. This recognition came about through the efforts and foresight of an industrialist and politician, the first Chancellor of the German Empire, Prince Otto von Bismarck (born April 1, 1815). On September 22, 1862 he was appointed Premier; prior to that he had been an ambassador to Russia and France.

The leading statesman of Europe introduced many firsts for the working man between 1883 and 1887. These included insurance against accident and sickness; old age pensions; and the limiting of child and woman labor. These changes became a model for most European countries. Bismarck died in 1898.

As of the end of 1981 there were 14,000 Americans who had reached the age of 100 (and over), so we can assume there are about 1,400 Canadian centenarians. In the United States, twenty million people have reached age sixty-five, and in Canada about two million.

INTRODUCTION

What This Book Is
All About

Are you forty? Sixty? Eighty? Retired, or thinking about it? Then this could be the most important book of its kind you will ever read!

I wrote it after I "presumably" retired, and after talking to seniors across Canada and in many parts of the U.S. while doing open line radio shows and talkshows on TV, I learned that many senior citizens have two main concerns. One was how to stretch the pension, and the other was how to get more interest out of life.

So this book, after much research, is designed to do two things for you. It will give you an opportunity to make a second income, or have a second career.

I have taken over seventy-five of the most exciting and proven plans I could find and described them just the way they were explained to me by the men and women who are operating them. Many of the plans can be worked from home no matter where you live, and many don't require much money to start. And best of all, you don't have to be a businessperson to make them work!

I discovered that the most successful retirees are often those who start planning for retirement long before they actually do. And in this book, you'll meet some of the most fascinating people you can imagine.

If you have worked out a plan, or have acted on any ideas from this book, why not drop me a line, care of the publisher. Who knows? Your idea could appear in the next edition!

R.J.C.

1

Let's Look at Retirement

Some people approaching retirement age regard their previous sixty-five years or so as a battleground on which a fight has long been waged but at last is ended. There will be nothing to do but lie in bed in the morning, maybe take that holiday they have long planned, get the garden in shape, repaint the house, put the stamp collection in order, and do a hundred other chores waiting to be done. Yes, they tell themselves, life is really going to change from now on. This is going to be living. But is it? Can someone suddenly stop doing the things he or she has been doing most of their life? It's a question many people are going to have to address.

Retirees come into the stream of life in North America at the rate of about a million a year. Canada now has two million retirees, and the U.S. has twenty million.

Whether we realize it or not, we are fast becoming a dominant force! And, by the year 2,000, the average life expectancy will approach eighty years.

Variations on Retirement

Some people retire at the recognized age of sixty-five (most of us do). A few take early retirement, while others stay on with the company until they feel they've had enough of routine business. A few have businesses of their own, and keep right on working and wouldn't do anything else. I've met all kinds of business owners. One has a weekly newspaper, another has an insurance business, some are in real estate, and so on.

Those in real estate, who entered after retiring from a nine to five job, say it's a great occupation. Younger real estate people have that glint in their eyes that says, "Got to make this sale. My own mortgage is coming up, or I want to get that new car, or the wife's bugging me to get out of this business."

But as one senior I met in Maui, Hawaii, last year said, "I'm selling real estate in a leisurely manner as it were. I have a couple of pensions coming in so it isn't a make or break deal. If I don't sell to the next client, I'll sell to the one after that. I can tell the prospects everything they ask me about bringing up kids, neighborhoods, and so on. They can tell I'm 100 percent sincere.

"I'm not out to do a million plus this year. Now I'm in the 'working-leisure' class and it's surprising how much business I do. I had hoped to sell probably one property during the first two months I was in the business. I sold three.

"I'm seventy-three now and making more money than I did working in a steel mill. I like meeting people, and this works out great. I can take a month or so off when it gets cold up north, like I'm doing now, and recharge my batteries."

This chap told me that the first month he retired, he left his alarm clock on to ring at six every morning just for the pleasure of being able to shut it off and go back to sleep. But he found that we still are all creatures of habit, and you just can't turn off something you've been doing every day of your life. And just because you've lived two-thirds or so of your life doesn't mean it's time to get out the old rocking chair, or join bus loads of retirees who play cards Thursdays, visit museums Fridays, and have dances on Saturday night. (Joe Smith's orchestra because he plays low and slow.)

Dr. M. Raff of Montreal, who is well up in his seventies and sees patients every day, said to me, "Retiring at sixty-five is like making an appointment with the undertaker. I've proved it many times that the longer you keep going, the longer you live. Only 'old' people retire."

Many people well past their mid-sixties are making important contributions to society. I recently wandered into the Van Dyck Photo Studio on Montreal's busy St. Catherine Street to have some publicity pictures taken. An agile white-haired man, whom I didn't know, shook my hand and then had an attractive girl take my name and deposit. A few minutes later I was being photographed by the same white-haired gentleman. When I complimented him on the obvious efficiency of the business, he relaxed for a minute and told me his name, which was Phillip Prosterman. He said he was seventy-four and had operated since 1932, and had no thoughts of retiring. "Retire?" he asked, "and sit around all day watching television? This is much more exciting and I'm doing something that's needed. Newspaper people, celebrities, all come to me to have their pictures taken. I'd be lost without my work. It keeps me young and keeps me busy."

There must be thousands of Phillip Prostermans around the world!

Plan your Retirement Career **Before** *You Quit Your Job!*

Most people plan their future when they reach a certain age or stage in life. This planning process frequently starts in the early teens with such questions as, "What kind of work will I get into?" In the early twenties, the question may become more specific, such as, "What type of company will I work for?"

A little later we may spend time pondering whom we may marry and where we will live. Then for the next thirty-five years or so we settle down, or most of us do, to a middle-of-the-road existence. Somewhere along the way we make a few investments which we hope, together with the pensions, will look after our physical needs when we retire. But what about our time and interest needs when we do retire? We seldom seem to plan for these aspects of our lives and yet they are extremely important. After all, we spend anywhere from a quarter to a third of our lifetime in retirement.

And we've spent a lot of time waiting for this happy day to arrive. One-third of our lives is spent working, one-third sleeping, and one-third messing around. If we had spent a little less time messing around, we might have arrived at retirement with a more complete plan as to what we are going to do in our remaining years.

Women Have It Easy?

Women don't seem to have the same retirement problems as men. Even if they've retired from a job, they still have the housework. And wasn't it a female who lamented, "A woman's work is never done."? And, of course, there are the long telephone conversations with the children and friends, and the shopping ... As one retired lady said to me, "I really don't know how I managed to take care of all my household and social duties when I worked. I can hardly take care of them now, and I'm retired."

But men are a different breed. The day they leave the job for good their whole lives change, although it may be some time before they realize it.

You Have to Have a Plan

A retiree without a plan is like a ship at sea without a rudder. Many of the retirees I know won't have the daily newspaper delivered. They walk to the store—it gives them something to do. Ostensibly they say, "I need the exercise." Many of them "forget" a second purchase as an excuse to make another trip to the store.

I have met some fascinating examples of retirees—hale, hearty, and vigorous—who were plainly bored with life. I asked a couple of chaps who were fishing off a dock in St. Petersburg, Florida, how the fishing was. One answered, "Hell, there's no fish here, but it's something to do."

While doing a phone-in radio show in Vancouver a woman called, and I could detect a note of desperation in her voice: "Can you suggest a little business my husband could start? He retired from his job six months ago. The first month or two he seemed busy enough, but now he spends half of his time in the kitchen. He wants to know what I'm cooking. Why don't I do this or do that. He's driving me crazy!"

After a lecture I gave, a man came up and said, "I'd like to get a copy of your new book as I'll be retiring at sixty-five in a few months. And I'd like to get one for Dad too. He's eighty-four, but always looking for something to do."

So apparently whatever our age, many people require a work plan if they are to live full, meaningful lives.

2

I've Retired Three Times

*Y*es, I've actually retired three times. Each retirement was an honest, calculated effort, but for some reason it never seemed to work out the way I'd planned it.

You'd think I'd had enough of working. After all, I started my first full-time job when I was eleven years old. I guess I wasn't a very good student. I barely made it into grade five and discovered I couldn't grasp long and short division, and decided I had had enough of school!

My father had "disappeared" leaving mother with no money, and the problems of raising the family. So the dollar-a-day salary I was paid by the local hardware store, as a delivery boy, certainly eased things at home. Anyway, it was a good excuse for a young fellow who didn't care much for school, and wanted to make his way in the world.

After some nineteen different jobs (I wanted to try everything) and a few small business ventures, I found myself, in the '50s, as owner and president of a small company that published three magazines: one for outdoorsmen, one for farmers, and one for sporting goods store owners. I had a staff of twelve. Two were college people, so anytime I was stuck for an answer I knew where to go. But the reverse occurred more often.

If you're in business for yourself, or planning a venture, remember that expansion can be as dangerous as no growth. In my case, by the mid-'60s, costs started to increase without the additional profit ratio I expected. I had to find an answer to the dilemma.

I Meet Joe of Chicago

I had been looking for a method of generating an overall

17

sales increase, so I went to Chicago to attend a publishers' convention. Might pick up some ideas, I thought. It was there that I met Joe at the Palmer House Hotel. He was introduced by a mutual friend, and his opening words went something like this: "I'm a remainder man. I deal in publishers' over-stocks."

I nodded.

"I can sell you good books at low cost. If an advertiser in your magazine cancels out, you can fill the space with an ad promoting one of my books. No cost for space. Boy, you could clean up."

Later, at the bar, Joe collared me. He put his hand on my shoulder and asked, "Have you ever run any mail order book ads?"

When I said I hadn't, he shook his head.

"You mean you publish magazines and you don't run book ads?" He looked at me as if I had just arrived from a Hudson's Bay Post by dog team.

"Everybody over here does it," he explained, ordering more drinks. He looked around, and then cupped his hand to his mouth.

"They sold a million copies of one of my titles. It's on memory training. Hardcover and a dust jacket. Sells for $5. I can give them to you at a dollar each. That's a $4 profit, but you'll have to hurry, I've only got a few hundred left, and *Life* phoned me this morning." He winked. "And when those big boys start showing interest in something it must be good. I just happen to have one in my briefcase."

He brought out a copy of the book and I had to admit it looked pretty good. Then he handed me a full page-proof of an ad.

"See that copy?" he asked. "Written by an agency fellow on Madison Avenue. And they know their business."

The ad explained that if you studied the book you could be introduced to all the patrons entering a theater and later, as they left, you could wish them all goodnight by name.

I told Joe I would try 300. Later, when I got to my room, I began wondering why anyone would want to say goodnight to a theater full of strangers even if you did remember their names.

The books had never been offered in Canada, and they might just take off. I often had some spaces to fill and I just might make some money doing it. The ad, except for a small picture of a Machiavellian-looking character, was filled with very small type, probably about the size of salt crystals.

My printer looked at the ad and laughed. "You expect anybody to read that? Set it over. Cut the copy in half."

I left the ad as it was. It was cheaper than resetting. Besides, I had long ago discovered that most experts "don't know nothing about nothing." I told the printer to put the ad on the inside back cover of the next issue.

The magazine wasn't out too long before some orders came in. There was cash, money orders, and checks. Not a lot of orders, about thirty-five, but it was encouraging.

I had a couple of girls in the office on circulation. They could fill the orders. It would give them something to do during slow periods. I juggled the ad in my three publications.

The 300 copies had arrived from Chicago. Canadian and U.S. money was around par in 1965, so there was no problem there.

Every day the mail brought orders. Once when I checked I found we'd sold 250 copies in the first eight weeks. Well, that was a thousand dollars clear profit. Not fabulous, but it might lead to something bigger.

Ed Sullivan Joins My Sales Force

One Friday afternoon, Joe phoned me from Chicago and excitedly asked, "Did you know the fellow who wrote our memory book was on the Ed Sullivan show? You'll sell a lot of books!"

I decided I would change the ad heading to read: "As demonstrated on the Ed Sullivan show!"

It didn't take long for things to happen. Book orders began to really move. I phoned Joe and asked him to rush me all the copies he had left—about five or six hundred. He said he would and casually mentioned that he had other remainders and recommended two of them. One was on growing hair if you were going bald, and the other was on how to be a professional fisherman. So we tried some advertising. I guess our readers had plenty of hair, but they must have been hungry for fishing information as the orders tumbled in for this one. Based on this success, I bought other titles from my good friend Joe.

Then I began to hear rumblings and grumblings. The girls were complaining that they couldn't get their regular work done. It seemed that they didn't like to work until 5 P.M. and then have to lug orders to the post office. And I was paying them a dollar an hour.

"Very simple," said Joe, when I told him I was having a little problem. "Do what the smart publishers here do. Put in a book department with full-time people."

So I gave this idea a try. Then one day I was talking to my bookkeeper about rising costs. "It's the book department," he said. "When there was no extra help it was a great moneymaker. But now ..." He shook his head.

Then I added another magazine, and took on two more ad reps. Now I discovered that I needed an ad manager to keep things moving. And as the total business increased it was necessary to have more office help. My C.A. explained there is a happy medium to sales and costs. We were just growing too fast, I guess. It was like my mother who had a boarding house. She was fond of saying, "You can make money with four boarders but, if you have five, you lose money." She would lean back in her rocking chair, sip her tea and explain: "If you have four, they can double up—sleep two in a room. You can buy food for three, add a little gravy to the stew, a bit more water to the soup, and of course you can always get an extra cup of tea from the pot. But take on a fifth boarder and all your figuring goes out the window. The fifth fellow has to have another room, you can't stretch the food so easily, you have to buy more, and there is more washing—and the price of soap these days ..."

So, when I had an offer to sell the business, I took it.

And then, for the first time in close to half a century, I was free from work. I decided to call it quits and retire.

But Soon I Was Back in the Saddle

Marriage councillors tell us that almost all men who get divorced are soon back in the matrimonial state again. I guess it's like that when you have a job. You might hate it at times, but once you're out you can't get back in fast enough. Like the chap I heard being interviewed on radio. It was his sixty-fifth wedding anniversary, and the interviewer asked, "Did you ever think of divorce?"

"Divorce never," said the man, "but murder many times."

Two weeks after I sold my business I got a copy (from an ad agency) of *Canadian Advertising Rates & Data*. This 500-page monthly is put out by Maclean-Hunter, Toronto, where I was once an associate editor on some of their business magazines. This directory lists just about every advertising medium in Canada: magazines, newspapers, radio, TV stations, and bus-stop benches. It's an education and, at the time of writing this, it sells for $25 a copy. I also borrowed the U.S. counterpart, *Standard Rates & Data*, 5201 Old Orchard Rd. Skokie, Ill. (60077). *Canadian Advertising Rates & Data* (CARD for short) lists all media in one publication but the American version has one book that lists farm and consumer magazines (650 pages), one for trade (business) publications, etc.

It is a common practice for publishers to check these reference books and see what might exist in the U.S., but not in Canada, and probably vice-versa. I soon discovered that there was a healthy business magazine called *Resort Business* operating in the States, but Canada, with its many resorts, had no similar publication.

So I immediately sent out a circular letter to advertising prospects to see if there was any interest. It cost me $50 including postage, letterhead (100), and typing. I'm a strong believer in doing a little survey before starting a business of any kind. Ask questions, write letters. The feedback will tell you a lot.

I wrote to firms who sell outboard motors, boats, air-conditioners, TV sets, furniture manufacturers, leasing companies, and others who would want to reach Canada's 5,000 resort owners. My first ad came from the old *Toronto Telegram*. Very encouraging—the back cover for the next five years! Why did they want it? They wanted to attract more advertisers to their classified resort ad columns. The *Globe & Mail* also signed up for advertising, but the *Toronto Star* showed less interest. Later I got some space from the *Toronto*

Sun and the *Montreal Star* and a Philadelphia paper. None of these people knew about me until then. It was all cold sales. But they liked the concept, proving that if you have a good idea and know how to present it, you'll get business. But the biggest advertiser of all for that first issue was Mercury Outboard Motors—an eight-page insert that almost paid for the printing of the magazine. A few months later I bought two business publications, then I got a fourth. I guess I was thinking of my mother's philosophy: "You can't make money with three boarders." I was back in business again in a big way for a little guy!

I discovered that the first time you retire it's like moving from a house you've lived in most of your life. But the second time, there doesn't seem to be that nostalgic feeling.

Whatever the reason, when an opportunity came along to sell my magazines, there was no hesitation. The sale was conducted overnight, and except for one typewriter (in case I wanted to write to some old friends as a way of passing a pleasant afternoon), a desk and a chair, from my very first venture (dry cleaning), an adding machine for totalling household bills, and two filing cabinets to keep them in, everything else was gone in exchange for a healthy check.

So now I was all set to retire, and the pensions would be along in a few months, which made it all the more logical.

How to Retire and "Un-Retire"

A friend, Charles Spilka, who formerly lived in New York, had retired from the mail-order business and moved to a suburban area. He has developed the knack of retiring, yet not retiring.

When he was in business (four book clubs), he used to buy names. This is a big business. Hundreds, maybe thousands of people all over the country work at it, from little girls with big machines to high-priced executives with bigger desks.

These people gather names—yours and mine. They buy them from magazines, from ads you may answer, catalogue houses, etc. These names are worth far more than the gold found in the rush of '98.

Do you want a list of pregnant ladies? One hundred thousand bicycle owners? School teachers? Women who buy by mail? You can buy a list (millions of names) for $30 to $50 and up per 1,000, all depending on how selective and how new.

Brokers, as they call themselves, advertise to people who sell by mail, and this includes an awful lot of names you'll find on the big board.

The people who sell the names usually send them on pre-glued labels, and the order usually specifically states "for one-time use only." Moreover, when you buy a list, you frequently have to agree you won't copy it. Many firms, such as most magazines, sell their names but won't let them go out of their hands. Some "list" houses put in a few dummy or house names to check on the customer's honesty. If this list is used a second time, the listing firm is soon aware of it and a customer might find it difficult to buy names in the future. The list, firms point out, is their business. If customers use it more than once, they are presumably doing so illegally.

In the case of magazines, you send them your material in envelopes, along with postage, and they'll address and mail. What are returns from such mailings? Three percent is about average, and 5 percent is considered miraculous for "cold mailings," as they are called.

There are dozens of list brokers, and some have been operating most of this century. If list brokers don't have a local office, they have reps like my friend Charles Spilka. But he doesn't work too hard at it. He's well-known in the business, and if someone in his locality wants a certain type of list, they'll probably call him. He in turn calls the broker who handles that kind of list (such as 10,000 farmers in Iowa or southern Ontario who haven't bought a new plough for five years) and the client soon has his names, and Charles his commission check.

He and I were drinking coffee one lazy afternoon, and I told him I hadn't done much of anything for at least three months. He said, "You've been writing for years. Why don't you write a little booklet on 'writing tips.' Maybe fifty to sixty pages, and sell it by mail for $3 or $4. You could print it for half a dollar."

A couple of days later another friend, Max Seeley, who is

with *Globe, Midnight* and *National Examiner* (tabloids in West Palm Beach, Fla., Rouses Point, N.Y., and Montreal), a classified ads manager, said that a few years back he had produced a booklet on how to make wine, which he sold by classified ads, and made about $100 a week. Then I heard of a girl who produced a digest-sized booklet on dozens of ways to cook hamburger and thus keep meat costs down. The last I heard it was doing okay.

I knew something about amateur photography, such as how to make money at it with simple equipment. So, I wrote and published a forty-four-page $3 booklet, "Twenty Ways to Make Money with Your Camera." Some of the photo magazines reviewed it, and the orders began to arrive.

I seemed to be getting busy all over again, and the fishing season was just opening. I decided that maybe a little early morning angling would be just the thing for a rest break.

Let's Go Fishing

When I published the outdoors magazine, companies were always sending me free lures, reels, and so forth, to try out, and of course write about. I did my share of reporting on the lures often in the hope of getting advertising, as all outdoor publishers do. And although I had given away dozens of samples (they make great Christmas gifts) I still had dozens left. So my summer vacation would be a great time to try them out. A fishing trip up north with a guide and a buddy would be just the thing. So, off we went. His car (I hadn't driven for years) and my boat and trailer coming up the rear. I knew a place on the Ottawa River where black bass were just waiting to smash into our bait.

We got to the lodge and settled in for two or three weeks of great fishing. The fish were there and soon we had pulled in all that we wanted.

About the tenth day my friend went to the village to get some supplies, and I took my camera and wandered around the farm that stretched out behind the lodge. I came across an old barn and found the lodge's owner, bending over a half-finished boat with a hammer and a handful of nails.

Before he had a chance to finish telling me that they cut the big pine on their property to build these beautiful boats,

I was shooting action pictures of the resort-owner-turned-boat-builder. Sure I'm on holiday, I told myself, but there were a lot of potential stories and photo sales just lying here waiting to be picked up, so why waste the opportunity?

I wrote the story when I got home and then went off to Florida. It was my thirty-fifth trip there so I had to be excused for my lack of enthusiasm, and this was also the main reason I didn't stay the full three months I had originally planned. Besides, it was cool so there wasn't much to do.

When my wife and I got back to the snow country I was delighted to find a check for my article and photos on the boat builder I had sent to a daily newspaper.

I still had plenty of boat photographs, and also some pictures of the lodge and owner, so I decided to write more articles. I think I spent close to a month on the next story. I sent the material to two boating publications, a fishing magazine, a resort (trade) paper, a handyman's publication, and various others. I was having a lot of fun and making money too. When I looked out the window and heard the biting north wind howling across my lawn, I just checked the oil gauge on the furnace and went back to work.

Come spring, and the work continued to increase. I was working hard again, but enjoying it.

Like Topsy this business had just grown, and I could see it getting bigger. Rates, of course, were going up as we got into the '80s. Many trade publishers were paying as much as $200 for 1,000 words, but it was demanding work, with tight deadlines. So I began passing assignments to fellow writers. A food editor asked for a piece on a potato-chip manufacturer. I passed it over to a correspondent I know and she said she came away with twenty large boxes of samples. In fact, she had to take a cab home, which cost her $8, but she passed the bill over to the editor who paid it. She probably listed it as transportation, which it was.

I then decided to concentrate on books. Deadlines were usually less hectic and there was more opportunity to express one's creativity. That would really enable me to slow down. So being a senior citizen, I decided to write about us, and I began to gather information on money-making ideas.

You will find examples of every kind. Some will appeal to

you instantly, others may have little appeal for you. Some of the ideas can be worked entirely from home, while others may be operated from outside, using your residence as a base. Some of the plans might be used as a springboard to other single, or multiple ideas. Some require limited capital to get started, while others require virtually none. Most of the ideas can be worked on either a full-time or part-time basis. These are decisions you will have to make for yourself. The important thing is that somewhere, someone is doing well with the ideas discussed here.

Some of the plans will enable you to make an additional worthwhile income. Others may result in a minimal amount of extra money. This depends on how hard you wish to work at your project. If you are like most retirees, there are days when there is no holding you back, while at other times you may want to just laze around. Most of the ideas presented can be worked that way. Once again, this is a personal matter with the final decision up to you. At least there is no boss carrying a big stick who is ready to put a pink slip in your next pay envelope if you don't conform to company standards.

So I hope you will read this book in a leisurely, thoughtful manner and get as much out of it as you can, and also that you will enjoy reading it as much as I have enjoyed writing it.

3

Working from Home Is a Tradition

When our forebears developed this land, they almost always started working from home, or very close to it. The blacksmith's shop was often next door, or if it was a retail establishment, chances were the family lived upstairs.

Senior citizens, too, will find it an excellent idea to work from home if they possibly can, and here are some good reasons.

The most obvious is that you eliminate the need for transportation. This saves time, money, energy, and the need to get all dressed up. You don't have to worry about the weather or where to go for lunch.

Other savings are utilities, rent, plus the hurly-burly of getting downtown by a certain time.

I have operated businesses from home on three different occasions, and I have worked out of all kinds of offices. No matter how you look at it, there is no place like home! It might give you a feeling of prestige to have an office, but except for certain types of businesses, it really doesn't matter as much as we think it does.

4

Photography and Journalism Were Made for Retirees

No book on how men and women retirees can make extra money, and have the time of their lives doing it, would be complete without a detailed report on photography and writing. Machines of all types have been invented to do all manner of things, but no machine can shoot a photograph for a publication and write the copy that goes with it. It's still a personal matter.

I have met retirees all over the U.S. and Canada who are living exciting lives as a result of photography and/or writing. A few were turning out novels, but most were free-lancing in pictures and copy.

The work is not difficult. I have had no particular training in the business, yet my short articles and photos have appeared in well over a hundred publications in the U.S. and Canada.

Recently, in the mail, I received checks totalling $310 for three photo pieces. One check was for five photos and a story on a local building supply dealer. He developed an angle whereby one of his staff will call at your house and tell you what you would require to renovate or build a new porch, repair some windows, build a shed, or other work. No charge for this service. Then, if you want the materials, the store will ship them over and you can do your own work. A great idea for handymen. The idea came from an ad I saw in the local weekly. Another check came from a story and two pictures about a firm which supplies automatic vendors and food to factories. The company installs up to six machines for hot drinks, hot meals, and frozen food. The employee takes a hamburger, spaghetti, or pizza out of the freezing compartment, drops it into the microwave oven and, in a couple of minutes, dinner is ready. The food firm fills their units daily. I never left the house (my basement office) to get this story. The company sent me facts and photos. Practically all firms (and people) love publicity, so getting cooperation is easy.

The third piece for which I received a check was about a lady who owns a travel bureau. It all happened quite by accident as many things do in the writing or "communications business" as I like to call it.

A small shopping center had a fire. No big deal, but fifteen businesses were affected by smoke and water damage. I saw the item in the paper and rewrote it for a business publication which carried news of shopping centers.

This, of course, was just the beginning. I think that old saying, "One man's meat, etc.," must have originated with journalists, because fifteen damaged businesses is fifteen stories when the places are refurbished, plus secondary rewrites to many other publications.

I filed away my first story and let the newspapers work for me by reporting any progress in the rebuilding plans. After a decent interval (like visiting the widow) I got the information operator at the Bell and asked for the number of the shopping center. When I dialed this number I got a very pleasant female voice. It turned out to be a travel agency. I had never visited this travel agency although it wasn't more than a few miles from where I live.

The lady explained she had just opened after having been closed for six months due to the fire, and she had been operating in makeshift quarters. But she had lost no business as a result of the problem. She also said she was a widow with two children, and before buying this business she had operated her husband's helicopter service after he had been killed in a crash. She gave me the story over the phone and had someone bring a photograph of her agency to me the next day.

This was a great story for a travel (trade) publication. And possibly one later for a general travel magazine, and certainly one for the Homestyle or Personality page of a daily. And this type of work could be great for people who, for one reason or another, don't care to leave their homes.

New inventions are forever helping people with little personal problems. I've had an eyesight problem for years. Focusing for sharp pictures is a problem for many people, including me. But the new cameras which focus automatically (Canon, Minolta, etc.), pay for themselves very quickly with their ability to enable you to point and shoot and get professional pictures in almost any light.

In communications you have a number of choices. You can spend your time taking photos (with brief captions) which you can sell to newspapers and magazines. Or you can forget the photos and concentrate on fillers (short articles) which are in constant demand. All this is simple enough assuming that you like this type of business and spend some time learning its intricacies. However, supplying photos with short, and sometimes longer articles (500 words or so), is relatively easy to do and is by far the most profitable. Many retirees are doing just this, and making out extremely well.

As an example of how one retiree got into this business I'd like you to meet Jason P.

Of limited education, he worked for a pulp and paper firm which was located on the outskirts of a small town. A few months before reaching retirement age, he began thinking of what he might do with his time. He had a couple of pensions coming, but if he could do something to stretch the pension . . .

It was then he decided on a new career, and that would be photography, something that had appealed to him, but which he had done nothing about. He was surrounded by lakes, rivers, mountains and animals; so there'd be no shortage of subjects to shoot.

Early on in his retirement, Jason bought a 35 mm Minolta camera SL (single lens) and enough equipment to fill two shoulder bags. He thought he might sell a few pictures in a month or so: it's great to have a hobby, but far more interesting when you get paid for your work.

Jason bought a few books on photography and also borrowed some from the library. Over the years he had taken pictures with an old Kodak, but as he said, he really never had time to develop the latent skill he knew he had. But now it would be different.

He was soon out getting photos of the darkening clouds, the sun rising over the hills, and the old churches in town. He even got pictures of his wife's cat "laughing." He sent these to the camera magazines, and even to *Woman's Day*, but they'd all come back.

Then one day he came across an abandoned hotel and a railway station near Rangley, Maine, left standing after a forest fire had roared through the bush country well over half a century earlier. Being constructed of field stone, the buildings were about all that was left of what had once been a small village.

The railway tracks had been removed for their steel back at the beginning of World War II, and there was the foundation of a stone house. All that remained was a pot-bellied stove with a fifty-foot-high tree growing out of its belly. Jason shot some photographs. At that point he couldn't figure who might be interested, because it wasn't anywhere near as pretty as his sunsets, and no one wanted them. But he had some film left in his camera so figured he might as well use it up.

Jason sent an assortment of the abandoned hotel and railway station pictures to a Sunday weekly. The pictures came back but so did a letter! "If you'd shoot in black and white (we run little color) and send us some background material regarding the fire you mentioned, we'd probably be able to use them. We pay a flat fee of $75."

Suddenly Jason's whole outlook changed. It wasn't the money so much, it was the fact that after being on the shelf he was now earning some money again.

He went to the library, and with the aid of the librarian found a considerable amount of material on the big fire. Acreage, date of fire, damage, etc. Then he put some black and white film in his camera (Kodak TR-X 400, 35 mm). He took a couple of seniors along to act as models. The station board which told when the New York night train was due was still in place, as was the semaphor, and Jason got photos of his two associates pointing. He'd already learned that action makes pictures come alive.

When asked by a friend the next day what he was doing

to pass the time, Jason said off-handedly, "Oh, I'm doing a little photo-journalism for a newspaper."

The librarian put him on to other possible markets for his fire photos. One was a forestry magazine, and the other a tabloid (newspapers buy for their immediate circulation area, so he could sell to other dailies). He also did a piece for an outdoors magazine which wanted a report on how the fishing and hunting were in that area. He had to get two fishing photographs and 500 words of background information. He wrote his copy the way he wrote a letter—just the facts. When the material came out he saw that his pictures were the same but his copy had been touched up. But he got his check and was happy.

Single Shots Sell Easily

One day Jason visited a small town and had his camera along (bus trips are excellent for this). The first thing he spotted outside a gas station was an old farm wagon filled with used tires. The owner said the wagon was built in 1910, but was still in excellent condition. A lot of people coming in for gas would get out of their cars and examine the wagon. Some would even stay to buy tires.

Jason took a photograph (black and white, of course, since most business magazines run no color), and also talked to the dealer—his length of time in business, how he got the wagon, how much the sales had increased as a result of this simple promotion.

An automotive publication bought this filler item for $20.

Then Jason came to a hardware store called the "Hub" and found it had a stand out in front of the store. This was about two feet by six feet and displayed odds and ends on sale. The main point was the two wheels on the display were replicas of old-time buggy wheels and were made by a New Hampshire firm which specialized in this type of thing. This display was so successful that the merchant was having three more made. In bad weather it is wheeled into the store and used to display certain lines such as holiday items. One photo plus information brought Jason $30.

Next, Jason got talking to a paint and wallpaper dealer who had sold a lot of paint and wallpaper over the thirty-five years he had been in business. He was still as active as ever with no thought of retiring. Jason got a picture of the exterior of the store, and one of the dealer, looking at some merchandise. (Try to get your subject doing something.) This piece (about a page printed) with two photographs brought $60 from a hardware publication. Total income, $120. About two days' work altogether.

Jason found trade journals a ready market. People read business papers to search for ideas they can use to make money, save money, train help, improve sales, and learn new advertising techniques.

Examine the type of trade journals in which you are interested. There are business magazines on any subject you want to mention: food, styles, children's wear, toys, industry, transportation, appliances, construction, clothing, travel, and so on.

If Jason noticed in a directory the name of a trade journal he might be interested in, he would write the editor for a sample copy. Sometimes he would get a worksheet of editorial needs and rates along with the magazine.

Most merchants get trade journals. (Many are sent free because publishers usually guarantee advertisers a certain circulation and can't depend on 100 percent paid subscriptions.) So your friendly merchant may have back copies he will let you have.

You won't sell every piece you submit, but as you gain confidence you might sell most of them. If you want rejected material returned, include a stamped, addressed envelope.

Over 15,000 Markets for Photos and Non-fiction
There are 1,775 daily newspapers in the U.S. and about 8,000 weeklies. In Canada there are 75 dailies and 800 weeklies.

Jason discovered that there were plenty of markets for photos, many of them paying $10 to $25 and more. For example, there are over 5,000 trade journals in Canada and the U.S. This is a very big market. Photos with cutlines, and sometimes features on retailers, manufacturers, and distributors, are in demand.

Jason's background was forestry, and he soon began capitalizing on his old trade by taking photos for the pulp-and-paper magazines.

He found that in addition to directories containing names of publications, the library (and bookstores) carried various writer's and photographer's market guides. These contain names of editors and publications, and also the type of material wanted and rates paid.

So, if you have any interest in photography and writing, why not follow Jason's example. There is a constant and growing need for editorial material. One reason is that the higher salaries paid to reporters means the more interested the smaller publications become in free-lance offerings. Free-lancers are usually paid less than salaried people (no holiday pay, pension plans, etc.) and offer coverage from different parts of North America with little or no travel costs to the publication.

Multiple Sales Pay Off

Jason learned from a writer's magazine that one chap had sent the same photo and story to forty daily newspapers and had sold twenty of them. The subject was on how to spot counterfeit money. This person simply contacted Washington for information on the problems merchants have with "funny money." (Some writers send out photocopies but most have more success sending out original typed pages.) Washington had sent him one photo and he immediately took a negative and had copies made. After all, he had paid for the original as a tax payer!

The author who had sold the twenty features (twenty-one if you count the piece he sold to the writer's magazine) was actually running a small syndicate from his home. This writer said that he received from $20 to $60 a story for a total of about $1000. The actual time involved wasn't much over a week as he had someone do his typing.

The writer/photographer who is going to make money at this business will try to sell a story as many times as possible. Some publications ask for world rights and usually pay more for the privilege. But there is nothing to stop you from doing a rewrite and selling the same piece as often as you can.

Ideas are public property. Their wording isn't. Many writers make a living going through old magazines in the library, updating stories where necessary, rewriting and sending out the piece.

I once came across a story in an old *Saturday Evening Post* in the Carnegie Library in Windsor, Ont. The feature was about strange and unusual invention ideas that the public sends to car makers (such as the suggestion that the front seats of cars be equipped with spittoons). I jotted down the ideas, then wrote the three big automakers for any unusual ideas they had received from the public. I got twenty ideas back, including four that had appeared in the SEP story. I wrote this piece and sent it to *Weekend Magazine* and got a good check almost by return. Come to think of it, it's about time I updated that piece again. Bet it will sell. Or would you like to try it?

A Steady Stream of Checks Every Day

I know people in free-lance photography and writing where seldom a day goes by that they don't get at least one check. Eileen S. tells me that a $1,000 a month for her material is normal, and she expects to continue producing well into her seventies, and maybe her eighties if she is still around.

On the other hand, I knew a man in Hamilton, Ontario, who wrote about some of his WWI experiences in 1920, and in 1970 he was still trying to peddle them. I visited him and he dragged a trunk out from his bedroom to show me his articles. I think the only thing he ever sold were a few neighborly news items to a local daily, *The Spectator*, for which he received two or three dollars and a coveted byline.

Why didn't this chap sell, and yet Eileen did? The answer is simple. Eileen wrote what the editors wanted. She telephoned and visited their offices. Queried them on ideas. She scanned the newspapers for ideas.

Two or three lines in a newspaper, such as a new business being opened, can, after taking photos and getting information, be fattened to a $200 photo-story.

So, if you have retired or are looking toward this happy day, why not start studying the publications which you intend to submit to. You will soon see what they buy in photographs and copy.

It's a great part-time or full-time occupation for seniors. I know. I've been doing it for years!

5

How About a "Ma and Pa" Motel?

For ten years I published a resort and motel magazine. At the same time, for a brief period, I owned a small motel in Fort Lauderdale. I didn't make much money out of the motel, but I did on the magazine. I found absentee management doesn't always work.

Owning a resort motel, especially if you are on your way to retirement, or have reached it, offers a lot of pluses, and a few negatives.

First, let's look at purchasing prices. Small places run from about $10,000 to $15,000 a room. Thus a fifteen-unit layout could cost you over $200,000. Prices obviously are based on location, quality of the building, and to some degree the furnishings. Furnishings are often leased by the operator. You choose the entire decor of the rooms. This may cost $2,000 per room or more, especially if you include TV and air conditioning. On a twenty-room layout you are looking at a $20,000 figure or more.

You sometimes see ads in the daily newspapers offering reclaimed hotel furniture at big savings. Often this is trade-in stuff that's been used for at least five years. That's the normal life of a lease.

Your leasing contract will cover the cost of furniture, interest, and any taxes. Payments will be on a monthly basis prorated over five years.

Here's How It Works

The main value of this service to a resort motel operator with limited cash is that there is often little or no down payment.

The leasing firm takes your paper to the bank (or other

money principal with whom he deals) and he gets his cash at once. You, of course, have to be a credit-worthy account.

Leases are for five years because by then the cigarette burns on the bureaus, and the cola spilled on the carpet are pretty evident. At this point you have paid off the lease. The leasing firm will allow you a small credit percentage, usually between 5 and 10 percent, if you start all over again, and this is usually done. Or you can keep your furnishings and the leasing firm will charge you a small outright payment. There are some variations to this practise. You are certainly paying more for your furnishings over the time of the lease than you would pay on a cash deal. However, you are getting installation, room planning, matching decor, even bedding and wall finishing. And your total cost for a small operation might only be $300 or $400 a month.

Figuring your annual income over a five-year period is difficult to do. Major hotels report that if they can get an average all-year occupancy rate of 70 percent they are doing well. In the first six months of 1982 for example, Montreal operators in the accommodation business claimed they averaged only 50 percent occupancy. You cannot make money on this ratio. Florida operators report 70 percent occupancy on the average. The larger operators get referrals from their chain members, travel agancies, and national advertising.

To arrive at your income, which at best has to be ap-proximate planning, you have to take into account weather, competition, economy, labor, taxes, and general operating costs.

I met a man in Fort Lauderdale who had originally been a farmer in Europe. He came to Canada where he eventually bought a 100-acre farm. It is difficult to make a good living on a 100-acre farm, but more land, if he could have got it, would have meant more labor. He was already working twelve and more hours a day.

A factory came along and offered him $100,000 for his spread. He didn't hesitate and his next stop was Florida.

My farmer friend arrived in Fort Lauderdale a couple of days before Christmas when the tourists were banging on motel doors at three in the morning begging for nonexistent rooms for which they'd pay any price. If you're in the mood to buy, and you find a scene like this, the chemical reaction in the body can be quite a potent force in helping you make a decision.

Our buyer found a motel for sale. Two blocks from the ocean. Twenty rooms and a pool. Twelve of the rooms were efficiencies. The price was $350,000. The owner was fed up with the long hours he was putting in, and so was his wife.

A real estate agent said that a popular buying formula in smaller motels is as follows: Try and buy a place where the annual income per room is at least $4,000 to $5,000. Then multiply this by the number of rooms. On twenty rooms you have $80,000 to $100,000. Next, multiply this by a figure between four to six times to get your buying price. On this formula you are talking $400,000 to $6,00,000. The former farmer, who paid $350,000, got in for slightly less than the $4,000-per-room formula.

With twenty rooms he needed three employees. If they did a proper job of cleaning they could do seven rooms each. But there was also the laundry to be done, halls to be vacuumed, and split-work on weekends. Then there was the outside work. He had a part-time man for garbage, pool maintenance, repairs to furniture, grass and shrubbery trimming, and painting. On top of this, the owner or his wife had to be close to the desk from 8 A.M. to 9 P.M. because the place was usually busy. People were checking in, checking out, just dropping in and asking questions, or picking up postcards for people who had heard about the place.

The first year he averaged $4,500 a year per room or about $100,000 including deals with travel agents for weekly travel tours, both bus and air. He had an all-around 60 to 65 percent occupancy rate. In his gross, he also had soft drink machines, the laundromat, and pinball machines.

On the $100,000 income, he figured $20,000 for staff; $23,000 for ads, business phone, electricity, taxes, pest spraying, leasing, accounting, purchasing supplies, and fire and damage insurance; and principal and interest would be $42,000. Total gross costs would run close to $85,000, leaving a profit of $15,000. Once the principal and interest were paid off, of course, the owner would do very well. He admitted that it wasn't a very good deal when you figured the hours you had to be on the job, but at least he wasn't shovelling snow.

His last remark as I left him was, "You know, there's hardly a day that there isn't someone at the door wanting to know if I want to sell the place. And I'll tell you honestly, I just may. That's where the big profit is!"

The Spring is the Time to Buy in Florida

Talk to any travel agent and you'll be told that fewer people travel to Florida in the spring than at any other season. This probably applies to Texas and Mexico and other places where Canadians go to get away from the cold. By April it's getting warmer at home, and travelers are returning. April and May are the best months to buy in Florida for the reason that there are fewer tourists and as a result resort income is lower.

It's psychological to some extent. If you walk into a little business on Toronto's Yonge Street that you had thought of buying, but the clerks are standing around looking at each other, your enthusiasm is bound to wane.

In Florida, especially southern Florida, you can wheel and deal more easily in the spring. The operator will pull out the figures for his high season, the winter, holidays, etc., but will often gloss over the spring, except for maybe a flurry around Easter. While real estate listing prices might not drop, and larger operators can afford to hold for their price, the small operator who wants to sell will often offer a better deal when his place is a quarter full.

Summer used to be a slow season, but now whole families go "south" and things boom then. The fall has become convention time, and many of the larger places report full occupancy in the fall. Golfers too like the fall in the south because the weather is cooler. All this has a direct or spin-off effect on just about every business, including smaller operators.

It is during this time that much of the due bill advertising appears. This is advertising in exchange for accommodation. There are advertising agencies that live off due bill ads.

Magazine publishers, newspapers, radio and TV stations receive circulars advising them that "here is a list of 500 or

1,000 hotels which they or their staff may stay at in exchange for advertising. The only payment is 15 percent of the total amount of accommodation taken." This payment goes to the agency for making up the ads and arranging the deal. Publishers often get these deals with chain motels. I have driven three or four thousand miles on a trip and stayed at the same chain throughout on a due bill, paying only the 15 percent and local sales tax, if any. Sometimes meals and bar are included. The offers apply to the Caribbean Islands, and sometimes to Europe and Mexico. Not all hotels offer this service, but there are hundreds of all sizes who find it worth exchanging otherwise empty rooms for advertising.

The Problems of Absentee Management
    I'd found a twelve-suite motel that was fully rented, so on the spur of the moment bought it. Then I boarded my plane, waved goodbye to Florida, and headed back to my home in Montreal. I had checked the property on paper. Everything worked out. How could I lose?
    I appointed a real estate firm who specialized in management of buildings. They charged 10 percent of the monthly income.
    The first inkling of trouble I had was when I received a 1,200 mile person-to-person call from the management division. They wanted me to rush $1,000 to them. Why? Because some drunk had overshot the stop line in my parking area and had hit the motel. In addition to removing ten square feet of stucco, he had hit a pipe, and water was gushing everywhere, including into a tenant's living room. I was only renting on a three-month or longer basis. No one knew who the offender was.
    The next call was for money to put up a new sign. I had an eight-foot-high metal peacock sign and some kids thought the sign would look better elsewhere.
    For the next three weeks things were great. I was almost at the point where I wasn't afraid to answer my phone. Then I heard the voice of doom. Actually, it was Millie from the management firm whom I'd come to know quite well. "This time we need $2,000 or the plumber and asphalt people won't do the work!"

"What work?" I asked, quivering with trepidation.

In my abysmal ignorance I had neglected to ask the owner or real estate salesman if the motel I was buying had city sewage. I guess they forgot to tell me because I discovered in the next ten minutes that my building was in a septic tank area, and the builder had placed the two large septic tanks under the center of the twelve-car parking lot. So not only did a good part of the lot have to be torn up, but considerable plumbing work had to be done on the installation if my tenants were to have facilities that worked. The matter that finally brought me to tears was when Millie phoned to say that this time she only needed $500. Someone had kicked in the beautiful pink louvred doors that lead to the laundromat machines. The reason? The town had closed off the water supply for a couple of hours to do some work. The laundro-mat doors had been locked as the machines wouldn't work without water.

At this point I decided to sell. The place was only five years old so there was no difficulty in shining it up and selling it.

6

Wouldn't a Little Fishing Resort Be Nice?

*I*f you've done much fishing, you've probably stayed at a camp.

While the mist was rising, the loons calling out, and the fish breaking the surface of the water, you stepped into your boat. You saw that the 10 hp motor was in place along with the gas tank. The bait looked okay, and you had brought your rod and tackle box. As you buttoned up your windbreaker against the early morning chill, the lodge owner gave your boat a push, and shouted that just off that island was a good place for bass. While your buddy got the motor going you opened your tackle box and wondered which bait to use first. Maybe a little spinning with a Flatfish might be the thing, so you attached your lure in anticipation. As you cast out, you wondered how nice it might be to own a lodge when you retire from the job.

Questions to Ask Yourself

A fishing lodge owner has to be a real outdoors type if he is going to be successful, and he'll be kept busy. His workday begins about 6 A.M. Outboards have to be put on the boats, the tanks have to be filled with gas and oil, and live bait has to be supplied. He must know who has rented the 10 hp, who the 15 hp, etc. He will require help in the busier seasons; a son of about sixteen is very convenient, but this has to be worked out in advance.

The owner will have to go to town a couple of times a week for supplies. Then there is the job of keeping the cabins supplied with firewood as it often gets cold up north, and guests like a little heat.

He'll have to be good at cleaning fish as most guests will

want their catch filleted, wrapped, and frozen. And the owner will be hoping that they catch their limit so they will advertise the lodge and also come back.

It will help if the operator is a good cook, because when he guides any parties they will expect a shore dinner.

A large garden will supply many of the vegetables so spare evenings will be spent weeding and doing other gardening chores.

Most Operators Figure Their Season from May to September
One operator I know has a lodge on the Ottawa River. The fishing is bass, pike, walleye and pan fish. He is open from June through to the end of September. Bass season opens about mid-June. He has six cottages, plus the main lodge, where the meals are served. He can take twenty guests, but during the sixteen weeks he is open he averages about twelve guests a day. His rates are $200 a week, boat included, motor extra. His total gross is about $40,000 a season. This would be about average as most fishing lodges are small operations.

Food is the big item (costs an average of 25 percent of income) and "Mama" supervises this. The owner's wife is often called "Mama," especially by the American visitors. Fishermen from across the border make up at least 60 percent of the traffic, and lodge operators love them. They come mostly from New York, Pennsylvania, New Jersey, Michigan and other bordering states. Lodge operators invest most of their advertising dollars in classified ads in dailies that serve these areas.

Help is important. My Ottawa River friend employs three women. Remember, he has a seven-day week, open seven to seven, and all labor laws apply.

In addition to cooking and serving meals there are the cottages to look after. Help is a problem. Most people don't want short season work. Some operators use college kids. They'll work for top money for eight weeks and often disappear weekends to do their own thing. A good liaison with a local couple is usually necessary.

The owner is a whiz on outboard motors too. They take a lot of punishment, but must work perfectly. That means a couple of spares are necessary. Motors are available on a three-year lease plan, so he pays only during the season. Gas and oil are a heavy cost, and as he is some distance from suppliers, a good stock of hardware, parts, and foodstuffs is necessary.

The End of the Season

So the last guest has left. It's October and the days are getting cool. In fact not only is there frost, but also a hint of snow. At the lodge owners' association meeting, the secretary says that a travel agency is offering a special group package for two weeks to Hawaii. You sure are ready for a holiday and "Mama" has been going all summer too.

First let's look at the figures and see how we stand. In fact we have to get them to the accountant to get ready for the tax man.

If the owner runs an average Canadian fishing camp, he might have taken in between $40,000 and $50,000 for the season. From this his expenses will run at least 75 percent, without salary. Costs include food, motor payments, taxes, business phone, help, repairs, advertising, new equipment, plus a hundred other items he should have receipts for.

If he ends up with eight or ten thousand dollars, he has done well. He's had his accommodation, but not free meals, as the government expects operators to include meals as revenue. But all in all it's been a pretty fair year, not as much as he probably made before retirement, and the work is certainly harder. However, he feels pretty good, and that's a plus. If he gets fed up, he can probably sell.

In fact, it's worthwhile thinking about selling, because as the years go by a considerable amount of upkeep will have to be done to the cabins.

You might care to contact the Associations listed on the next page for details on the tourist accommodation business.

Bill Morrison,
Accommodation Motel
Ontario,
c/o Otonabee Motor Inn,
P.O. Box 366,
84 Lansdowne Street East,
Peterborough, Ontario.
K9J 6Z3

(705) 742-3454

Roger Liddle,
Executive Director,
Northern Ontario Tourist
Outfitters,
P.O. Box 1140,
North Bay, Ontario.
P1B 2T9

(705) 472-5552

Geoffrey P. Davies,
Ontario Motor Coach Assoc.,
c/o Charterways
Transportation Ltd.,
P.O. Box 847,
London, Ontario.
N6A 1H3

(519) 679-9150

Lin Winkelmann,
Northern Ontario Tourist
Outfitters,
c/o Winkelmann's Camps,
P.O. Box 237,
Sault Ste. Marie, Ontario.
P6A 1Z0

(705) 949-6100

Russell Cooper,
Executive Director,
Ontario Hotel & Motel
Association,
Suite 601,
10 St. Mary Street,
Toronto, Ontario.
M4Y 1P9

(416) 961-8440

Edward Seal,
Resorts Ontario,
c/o Glen House Resort,
P.O. Box 329,
1000 Island Parkway,
Gananoque, Ontario.
K7G 1V9

(613) 659-2204

Vic Henderson,
Executive Vice-President,
Accommodation Motel
Ontario Association,
P.O. Box 1563,
140 Braidwood Avenue,
Peterborough, Ontario.
K9J 1T8

(705) 745-4982

NOTE: In many areas outside of Ontario, resorts and motels are classified with Hotel Associations. To acquire information on resorts and motels, it is suggested you check with the hotel association serving your area. This information as to location headquarters may be acquired from your telephone operator, or local hotel manager.

7

Harry's Retirement Party Was a "Reel" Success

"Looking back over my initial retirement," said Harry B., "it reminds me of a bad dream. On Friday the staff at the office gave me a party. There was the usual drinks, food, and jokes. I do a bit of fishing, maybe twice a year. I think I paid $3 for my rod at a garage sale five years ago. But everyone had obviously chipped in to get me a gift. One of the girls had been sent out to choose it. I can imagine the conversation: 'Oh, old Harry likes fishing. Why not get him some tackle.'

"And tackle it was! They'd got me a jewel-bedecked level-wind reel. Well, just about everyone uses spinning reels today. The thing wouldn't even fit my rod. And I bet it cost $50. I'd have felt like a fool using it. Actually they could have got me a complete fishing outfit for less than the $50 they had paid.

"I had to give a big smile and thank them all. Before everyone left, I tried to find out who had bought it. If I could only gotten a hold of the bill. . . .

"But it turned out that little 'do-a-good-turn-for-anyone Nora' had performed the deed, and she and her boyfriend had gone away for the weekend."

Harry said he would have been much happier if the boyfriend had got the reel and he had gone away with Nora.

Retirement Starts . . .

The following two days, Saturday and Sunday, Harry was used to being home anyway, and Monday wasn't too bad. He did some weeding in the garden and kept thinking it must be a holiday of some kind.

But by the fourth or fifth day he began to feel like an astronaut who had been left on the moon by mistake. He must have passed his wife a dozen times in the hall. Sometimes he'd be on his way to the bathroom, or other times to the kitchen to get some pop from the fridge. He and his wife didn't bother to talk much. They'd talked about everything, except what was happening at the office. He felt like phoning a couple of times, but then felt it would be better not to. People he had talked to since retiring said the same stupid things. "Boy, it sure must be great. Nothing to do, just lie around all day." He used to be annoyed at the telephone in the office and its constant ringing. Now he'd jump at the first tinkle. Usually it was for the wife. He guessed no one knew he was home for good yet.

About two months after retiring Harry thought he might look for a job. But he soon discovered that there really wasn't much around. His own firm wasn't looking for any part-time workers.

It was then that Harry decided that maybe he could start a little business on his own. He would have to do something that would get him out of the house a good part of the time. He didn't play golf, and if he met an old friend on the street, it seemed that he was on his way to work, and didn't have time to stop and talk.

Harry had some friends who had retired and seemed perfectly content. One chap had bought a Volkswagen van and was always on the road. During the winter he and his wife would go to Texas or Mexico, and in the summer they were roving around Northern Ontario or the Maritimes. But Harry was only happy when he was doing something.

One morning he thought he might go out on the river fishing. He got his expensive reel out and decided to buy a new rod to go with it. So he walked down to the hardware store and spent $12.95 on a fiberglass rod. On the way out of the store he remembered he had no bait. In answer to his question, the hardware man said he didn't sell live bait, such as worms. When Harry asked him why not, the chap said he guessed it was because no one had ever offered him any. He admitted he did get calls for worms from time to time.

The lack of worms at any place Harry tried gave him an idea. Why couldn't he start a wholesale worm business? He remembered reading about a chap who was making $15,000 a year selling worms. He wasn't sure where he'd seen the article, but it was probably in one of the newspapers. The fellow mentioned in the paper dealt only in dew worms or night crawlers. He got them from golf courses. Golf courses didn't want worms raising humps on their greens, so they usually gave permission to people who wanted to pick them. Harry remembered that the pickers started work about 5 A.M. That was when the grass was moist and the worms were lying on the surface.

Harry soon learned that handling worms was a scientific business. The live bait is packaged in small cartons in lots of one and two dozens. The cardboard covers should have air holes, and the biggest mistake was putting worms in wet earth in cans or glass. These containers get too warm, and worms drown or become soggy in muddy water. Like pet cats and dogs, they have their own likes and dislikes. Keep worms properly and they will live a long time, and catch a lot of fish. They must be happy and agile.

Harry also learned that sphagnum moss is one of the best beddings in which to keep worms. Do not keem them in the trunk of a car, except for brief periods. When not being transported, keep them in the refrigerator, but not too close to the freezer section. Personally, I have often sneaked a box of worms in the back section of the fridge, until my wife found out. If you keep the boxes covered they will not escape.

Harry soon realized that bait shops and sporting goods stores that sell worms had refrigerators so he too bought an old one for $25. Once he got going he found that it was too small. Worms packed in moss require more room than those packed in worm compound. This is a chemical that is greyish black and comes in rough pellets, somewhat like grape nuts. This material beds and feeds the worms, and it doesn't dry out very quickly. Most commercial bait people use it. Check magazines like *Sports Afield* and *Field and Stream* and you will come across some advertisements for the pellets. Sporting goods stores can probably advise you where to buy them.

Harry found that there were plenty of retail outlets for worms. The best ones were gas stations along roads leading to fishing areas. He was soon calling on accounts and happy in his new profession. Hardware and sporting goods stores were good, and he even managed to place his stock in some convenience stores. He worked on both the outright sale method and on consignment deals. His biggest problem was getting stores to place the worms in a cool place, so he called at least every second day on his customers.

His business was primarily from April to October, but in some areas where there was ice fishing, he did manage to do a little business in the winter. A type of worm sold in the winter is a red manure worm. These worms are sold by the pound to gardeners, parks, and other public places for earth cultivation.

Worm farmers use trays of worms which are kept in cool places, such as garages. Trays are moved to different levels as the worms breed and grow. They are fed regularly and require a considerable amount of space. Harry learned of one worm farmer who had made a deal with a small city. They could dump all the city's garbage on his farm (excluding cans and bottles) and he in turn would use it as worm feed. He used to plough the garbage into the earth where worms were dropped, and they thrived. Sales of millions of worms to parks were not unusual. This farmer also sold to fishermen and wholesalers (by mail).

The mail order business can be a very profitable operation, because you have regular customers. Some fishermen order every week or two throughout the season.

There are books and vertical file papers on earthworm culture, so, if you are interested, check out your library.

There have been many baits invented hoping to copy the lowly worm, but I know of none that have succeeded. I have a four-pound smallmouth bass mounted in my billiard room that was taken on a little old red worm, and what a thrill that was!

8

Baby Brother Irving, at Sixty-Seven, Is Planning Big Things!

Walk into Bens Delicatessen in Montreal, and although there are 150 employees working there, chances are you'll be greeted by one of the three brothers who own the place: Solly, 78; Al 73; and the baby, Irving, who is 67.

Bens has been toddling along since the father, Benjamin Kravitz, started the business in 1908. The business has acquired an international reputation for smoked meat, but it's only in the last few years, when the boys "came of age" as they say, that the business has really started to expand, proving that you can get better as you grow older.

The Kravitz's invented the smoked meat sandwich according to gourmet history. Back in the old days in Europe, people used to pickle briskets of beef in brine in order to preserve it for winter eating. Mr. Ben, Sr., had developed a recipe that is still a family secret. When he opened a little store on Montreal's St. Lawrence Boulevard, he decided to specialize in smoked meat sandwiches. Thick, hot, juicy slabs of smoked meat between slices of freshly baked rye bread. The price in those days was a nickle a sandwich.

The three Kravitz brothers say they were weaned on smoked meat sandwiches. And they still enjoy them for lunch practically every day.

In the '70s, they decided that more people should have the opportunity of enjoying their delicacy. It wasn't a case of making more money, it was more a matter of sharing Bens with the rest of the world. So after the big noon rush was over, and all the tourist busses had left, and the businessmen had gone back to work after their epicurean feast, the boys would sit down quietly for a big sandwich and a little family business discussion.

Irving, being the youngest and president, would start off the conversation with, "More people should enjoy our smoked meat. You can't get too much of a good thing."

Solly, who used to be a professional wrestler a half century earlier, would nod in agreement. Al, who takes time to make a decision (he got married when he was 70), said, "I think I have an idea. We can sell a lot more smoked meat by having other restaurants sell it."

"So what else is new?" asked Solly. "We already got stores selling it."

"But how many? I mean lots," replied Al.

"It's a good idea," said Irving. "Not a dozen stores, but maybe in every city in Canada."

So while most men of their age are in the midst of retirement, the Kravitz boys were planning one of the biggest moves of their career. And within a short time the idea began to bear fruit.

First of all, restaurants everywhere, except in Montreal, were invited to buy smoked meat, dill pickles, and rye bread at wholesale and serve it to their customers. Soon restaurants began sending in their requests. After careful screening, about 100 were selected. Along with their regular menu, these chosen ones could offer Bens smoked meat sandwiches, and soon Air Canada was rushing the delicacy to eateries from Victoria to St. John's.

Once the cross-country program got going, the boys came up with further expansion ideas. The next step was to package smoked meat and put it in the meat display cases of Dominion Stores, one of the largest chain of supermarkets. Now millions of people would have the opportunity of enjoying Bens' specialty.

Once again the boys got together for a little think-tank session. Then the brothers came up with the most shattering idea of all. The statement came out almost as a chorus. "Why not offer franchises for Bens restaurants across the country? We could be the McDonald's of the smoked meat business!"

Soon the brothers were working overtime. What kind of unique buildings would be erected? Where were the best locations? Would other Bens products be sold?

"We have good stew," said Solly.

"Not unique enough," commented Al. "Stew doesn't have personality."

But as the months went by the blocks fell into place. There were meetings with architects, lawyers, city councils and, of course, a whole string of investors who wanted to get in on the ground floor.

So by the time you read this, there could be a Bens franchise opening near you. And, if you could manage to slip into one of their hygienically clean kitchens, you just might be lucky enough to see one of the brothers lifting the lid off a steaming cauldron making sure that the spicing of the brisket was up to Bens' standards.

9

A Novel Way to Take a Cruise

Jack Dunham was born in Los Angeles, but has lived in Canada for many years. When you chat with Jack you never think of a seventy-three-year-old retiree, and he never thinks of himself as one either. That's because he's always planning for the future.

When I talked to him in 1982 he was making plans to take a cruise around the world. Not the leisurely cruise of the retired millionaire with nothing better to do, but rather a working cruise of an ambitious young fellow looking for adventure.

Jack has many talents. He is tall, blond, handsome. He once was a set designer in Hollywood, and later an artist with Disney World. But his newest adventure is doing caricatures of tourists on board cruise ships.

I was having coffee with him at a restaurant. He had a stack of table napkins in front of him, and was busy scribbling. "Let's see now. I'll charge $50 a portrait, about thirty inches by twenty inches. I can do at least four, maybe five a day. I can do all right. And I'll spend a few days in South America, stop off in Africa, and do Spain, England, and probably go to Holland and Denmark. It'll be a lot of fun, and I bet I'll come home with twenty-five grand!"

It was the dead of winter, he was leaving shortly, and you just knew he'd succeed. He had the enthusiasm of a man half his age.

Successful deals were nothing new to Jack. Not so long ago he noticed a vacant lot on the corner of a main street of a small town. The lot had a "For Sale" sign on it. The area was about twenty miles from the city.

Our adventurous friend contacted the owner of the lot and

55

explained that he would like to rent it for a few months. A price was agreed upon, and Jack immediately placed a classified ad in the local papers announcing that he would "sell your trailer for a small fee." He began receiving phone calls at once. People with house trailers, campers, and similar units were interested.

Jack's plan was very simple. People would leave their trailers on his lot. They would tell him how much they wanted, and also give him their telephone numbers and addresses. At the same time, Jack began running ads announcing he had trailers for sale.

His usual charge was 10 percent. He'd suggest that the owner keep the price as low as possible in order to make a fast sale. If a prospect came along and made an offer less than the asking price, Jack would phone the owner and ask him if he was interested. Sometimes the owners would go along with the lower price, sometimes not.

Within a short time people began bringing in boats, and boat trailers. Jack ran the "lot" all summer and said he did very well.

During another period, and on another lot, he thought he might try selling cars. This was new to him, and he decided to try a new twist.

It was close to Thanksgiving, and he offered free cars with every turkey you bought. This idea was devoted primarily to cars five to ten years old. Sales prices ranged between $400 and $2,000.

Jack's ads read, "Buy your turkey from us, and we'll give you a FREE car!"

In other words you might pay $500 for a turkey, and get a nine-year-old Ford. People brought in their cars and often they stayed with them and made their own sale. Jack had arranged for a finance man to be on the spot to handle any financing. Jack charged 10 percent on sales. He said to me, "People were bringing in their cars to sell on one side of the lot, and the customers were driving out the other side with their free cars and turkeys."

The only thing Jack supplied was the sales area, a little advertising, and, of course, the turkeys. The birds, by the way, were live!

10

Grandma Makes It Big with Ice Cream

*I*n the fall of 1975, pedestrians and drivers on Fort Lauderdale's plush North Ocean Drive became aware of a strange phenomenon in their midst. On this busy highway, flanked by luxury hotels, condominiums, and apartments, there appeared a unique vehicle. It moved with the stream of traffic, and everywhere it went it created tremendous interest.

The vehicle in question was a 1901 Oldsmobile truck. Its full length was about as long as the hoods of the big cars it was keeping pace with. The little truck, with its beep-beep horn, wended its way in and out of traffic, and displayed on its panels in gold letters, the words GRANDMA'S HOMEMADE ICE CREAM. This was the first appearance of many that this museum piece would make in the months ahead. One year later it was estimated that this little good-will vehicle had travelled 25,000 miles in its task of publicizing Grandma's Ice Cream.

At first glance, one might think that Grandma's Ice Cream was a spin-off from one of the multinational corporations. But not so.

I made my way to 3404 North Ocean Drive, Fort Lauderdale, Florida, which is just a stone's throw from the ocean. Here I found Mrs. William Paisner behind the counter of a store which measured about fifteen feet wide by thirty feet deep. She was "Grandma," and she was busily scooping her ice cream into paper cups for waiting customers.

Mrs. Paisner told me that she came from Brookline, a Boston suburb. Her husband, Bill, had been in the plumbing business. She said, "About a year ago I decided that I would like to live in Florida. The main reason was that my married daughter had moved here, and she had just had a baby and

57

I wanted to see the little fellow grow up. Of course, I had no objection to getting away from the cold weather either. Bill and I would have to have an income so I began thinking about just what we might do.

"It seemed to us that making and selling ice cream should be pretty good, because after all the weather was hot most of the time, and that meant there should be a big demand for a high-quality, old-fashioned-type product. I mentioned the idea to my husband and to my son-in-law who was visiting us. In no time at all he came up with the idea that I should call it 'Grandma's Ice Cream,' and make it right in a store window with small freezers."

While Mrs. Paisner was busily engaged in selling ice cream, I glanced around the small store. It had half a dozen round tables, each with four chairs. They were the old-fashioned type made with copper wire which used to be so popular. Overhead hung a large Tiffany lamp.

"Business has been rushing since the day we opened the doors in November of 1975," she said. "Once we had the name 'Grandma's,' everything else seemed to fall into place. I had an instinctive feeling that everything was going to work out O.K. My husband and I began learning something about the ice-cream business, and then we came down to Lauderdale to look for a store. We found this one," she said, looking around. "It certainly didn't look the way it does now. The building is relatively new, but there were holes in the walls and the place was dirty. We cleaned it up and then bought some wallpaper with pictures of the '90s and old prints.

"The next step was to get a couple of old-fashioned ice-cream freezers, and put them in the window. Each one produces about twenty quarts a day, and I'll tell you that was hard work, but it attracted a lot of attention. Before long we had to go to a big, modern machine which turns out forty gallons a day. We decided that everything would be the best quality, and only fresh eggs, cream, and butter were to be used. Why, we even mash our own bananas for banana ice cream! "This is a busy spot—I figured this would be a good location, and even though the rent is $500 a month I took a five-year lease. I was a little scared at times, but now I know that I did the right thing."

Trade Can be Helpful

Mrs. Paisner said that the suppliers, manufacturers, and distributors were very helpful. She went to these people and learned as much as she could about the business.

"I found out," said Mrs. Paisner, "that there was a man in Chicago making old-fashioned ice-cream-store fixtures from the actual moulds from which they were made at the turn of the century. I was able to get fast delivery on these, and about a month after I came down here we were open for business. In fact, sales have been so good my husband decided to put his plumbing business back home up for sale. Then we sold our house in Brookline and bought a place here in Fort Lauderdale. We figured that we would have to scrape up about $25,000 to get started and I guess we spent all of that."

Mrs. Paisner said that about two weeks after they had opened the store, they were out driving around and they saw the 1901 Oldsmobile displayed at a service station with a 'For Sale' sign on it. "We paid a little under a thousand, but I wouldn't sell it now for $10,000. It's become a great merchandising idea. It brings people in from all over town. They say, 'We saw your truck and we just had to visit your place!'"

This is the type of promotion that makes professional PR men green with envy. "I guess it's just one of those things," commented Mrs. Paisner. With no merchandising experience at all, she came up with this tremendous idea. The family uses the little truck to go shopping, to dinner, and run messages.

Mrs. Paisner says she has been approached many times by people who want to open up "Grandma's Ice Cream" stores in the big cities on a franchise basis. She says that so far, while she has thought of this, she hasn't done anything concrete about it other than to register the name. One thing she is sure of, and that is if there ever is a franchise deal, or branches, an old-time vehicle will play a prominent part in spreading the name.

Talk About Publicity

Mrs. Paisner is a whiz on publicity and could probably get a job in the business if she ever wanted to. She wrote to me a year ago saying that she and her husband were going to drive from Florida to California in the little truck. And they did it. Newspapers along the way stopped her for interviews and, of course, photos. She and her husband appeared on radio and TV unceasingly. "The only problem," she said, "was the steep hills. Sometimes we had to get a push. But it was a wonderful holiday."

The Paisners put the little Olds on a train, and they flew home. "We hated to leave her," she said, "but the truck got home all right and I think she was glad to see us."

11

"Jack Rabbit" Johansen
Tells How He Reached 108

You can talk to medical people who may give you tips for living a long life, but your best sources of information are those who *are* living long lives.

One of these is Herman Smith, better known as "Jack Rabbit" Johansen. He was born near Oslo, Norway on June 16, 1875. So he's well over a 100 years old; in fact he's 108 and lives alone in the town of Piedmont in the Laurentian Mountains of Quebec.

Dr. Jack (he has an honorary degree) has three main rules for a long life: eat right, sleep right, and get plenty of exercise. And, of course, keep your interest in living high.

Jack's heaviest meal is his breakfast. Steaks, chops, and vegetables or stews are a regular part of his 6 A.M. breakfast. He says, "Before you take the car out for a long trip you make sure it is gassed and oiled. You should do the same with your body. The day's heaviest work is ahead of you." He cooks by wood on an iron stove in his cabin, and cuts his own wood.

For lunch he'll have a sandwich and soup. He drinks sparingly of tea and coffee, and has a little wine with his dinner, which usually consists of a salad.

Skiing is the big thing with him and in winter he skis four miles to the post office to get his mail.

By the age of twenty-four he had a degree in engineering and he was on trouble-shooting assignments going around the world for a U.S. firm. In 1900, an assignment with the old Grand Trunk Railway brought him to Montreal. In 1907 he set up his own engineering business and did well until the 1929 crash wiped him out. He loved skiing and with his wife, Alice, and three children, found an inexpensive cottage in the Laurentians. He reports that at one low period, the family existed solely on cabbages for weeks. But the depression was a godsend to him, he says. He began holding ski seminars and organized ski clubs in twenty-three mountain towns.

He has received many honors and was recently (1982) elected a member of the Canadian Sports Hall of Fame. One of his earlier achievements was to build the famous eighty-mile Maple Leaf Ski Trail, which winds through the Laurentians.

Brian Powell, who wrote a book about Dr. Jack, was visiting him and was shown a letter inviting him to appear on CBC's *Front Page Challenge.* "Why don't you go?" said Brian. "You'll enjoy it and the honorarium is good."

"Maybe," said Jack. He picked up a sheet showing photos of the four people who would be on the panel. "Jack Rabbit" said he thought the only one who might give him any trouble would be Gordon Sinclair.

On the occasion of "Jack Rabbit's" one hundredth birthday, he appeared on the show and Sinclair asked him what his secret was for reaching such a venerable age. Without hesitation "Jack Rabbit" answered, "If I tell you, you'll write a book about it and make a fortune!"

At this, the audience broke into gales of laughter.

Dr. Jack is still in demand, both to receive honors, and as a public speaker. But his daughter, Dr. Alice Johansen, a professor at McGill University, shields him from the public and today turns down any speaking invitations.

He still lives alone in Piedmont and enjoys cooking, although he does dine frequently at his daughter's. He still loves his independence.

12

Joe Always Got Elected

Another public figure, now eighty-one but still active, is Joe Smallwood, former premier of Newfoundland. I met him by chance in the late '40s and have since followed his career with interest.

I was sharing a small office with Ewart Young. He had just started to publish a Newfoundland magazine, the *Guardian*, and I was all excited about my new (and first) publication, the *Canadian Writer & Editor*.

In both cases the pennies had to be watched. I stayed in to answer the phone when he had to go out, and vice versa. Besides, someone might come in with an ad. Even a classified was welcome.

On this day, it was about ten in the morning and we were both working at our desks, when there was a knock on the door and it opened. My friend got up and said, "Hello Joe! What are you doing in Montreal?" Subsequently I was introduced to Joe Smallwood from Newfoundland.

Luckily we had an extra chair. I went out to the coffee stand on the main floor of the St. Catherine Street building and soon we were huddled around listening to Joe.

It seemed that Newfoundland would soon have the opportunity of becoming Canada's tenth province if it wished, and Joe had come to Montreal for a little rest and to think over whether or not he should enter the race for the premiership. He fervently hoped that Newfoundland would join Canada and he would be elected its leader.

Joe had, among other things been a "barrel-man." A "barrel-man" is the fellow who perches in a barrel atop a ship's mast and calls out when he spots something such as a whale, iceberg, etc.

But Joe had carried it a step further. He'd become a "barrel-man" on a Newfoundland radio station. There was little contact with the outlying areas, and it was Joe's job to inform listeners of births, coming marriages, and other news.

"You're well known," my friend said. "And they like you. You'll win."

Joe wasn't so sure. He'd been running a pig farm and selling his output to the American forces stationed there. He said it was profitable because he was able to get the scrap food from the base and he fed his pigs this. Probably one of the first recycling ventures.

We discussed publicity, promotion, but mainly Joe's chance of being elected. An hour later he got up from his chair, thanked us for our encouragement, and was off. Not too long after the press carried the news, "Smallwood to run for Premier of Newfoundland!"

And he was premier for twenty-three years. It is reported that an elderly lady, meeting Joe on St. John's Water Street, said, "Thank heaven we're part of Canada. I don't think I could stand another Newfoundland winter."

At the age of eighty-one Joe was Newfoundland's newest publisher.

He began writing and publishing encyclopedias about his beloved island in a little cottage on Portigal Cove Road in St. Johns. Sales weren't what he hoped they'd be and, when I last heard of him, he had borrowed a trailer and was out in the countryside selling his books house-to-house.

"It reminds me," he said, "of when I was a boy selling newspapers."

13

Mrs. Beck, Eighty, Is Chairperson of a Firm with $80 Million Sales

Many people wonder if they are too old to go into business. The success story of Theresa Beck is a good answer to anyone who wonders if age is a barrier to success. At eighty years of age, she is past-president and now chairperson of the board of Noma Industries Limited, Scarborough, Ontario. This firm and its associated companies are doing over $80 million a year in sales. In addition to Christmas tree lights, they manufacture artificial trees, snowblowers, and other products. The company has sales offices across Canada and in many parts of the world.

Said one Noma employee, "There are over 300 people at the Scarborough plant and they all adore Mrs. Beck. If a machine breaks down you may find her apron-clad with a screwdriver making it tick again. She is a very hard worker and her employees are equally dedicated." She calls them her family and long-time employees bring in relatives and friends as hopefuls when job opportunities come up. And, of course, she gets invited to "family" christenings and weddings.

In 1963 Mrs. Beck arrived in Toronto where she had a brother. She and her son Tom had left Hungary twelve years earlier and had spent the intervening years in England. Mrs. Beck wanted her son to get an education; he took up electrical engineering, and graduated with a degree.

In Canada, Tom went into the electrical business in a small way, and the company was named Beck Electric. A little later, a company called Noma Lites Ltd. came up for sale. (It was reportedly losing money.) Mrs. Beck and her son made arrangements to buy it.

Mrs. Beck admits that she had to watch every penny and

65

work around the clock, but soon the company began to show a profit and before too long the firm went public and Noma's name appeared on the Toronto Stock Exchange board. Their diverse companies are under the name Noma Canada Inc.

Age means nothing to Mrs. Beck who believes that if you keep working at something you find interesting, advancing years won't worry you.

14

Can Drive ... Will Travel

I recently met Howard M. on the beach at St. Petersburg, Florida. It was a raw day, and few people were strolling on the sand. I began talking to this man who, like me, was watching the construction of a building.

He was eager to talk and I was surprised when he said he was seventy-four. I learned his hometown was Alliance, Ohio, and he had retired from the fire department nine years earlier.

Howard said, "I soon discovered that a bottle of beer and a TV ball game aren't enough. A person needs a challenge. So I developed a second career and a second income. Driving cars."

He told me he enjoyed driving and he discovered that many people who holiday away from home like to fly to their destination but need their car when they get there.

It is generally agreed that older people often take better care of cars, and generally have considerable free time. This senior citizen let it be known around legal, medical, and executive levels that he was available to drive cars.

His rate is $30 a day, plus overnight hotel, meals, gas, and return air face. He says within a month he had a couple of calls, and soon, what with repeat business and word-of-mouth advertising, he had all the business he could handle.

Just about every town offers opportunities like this. A circular ($10 for 250 copies at most copy centers—you supply the original) will bring phone call enquiries. Normally, as you will be driving a person's car which is insured, you are covered too, but check this out.

If you don't want to print à circular, have a few business cards made up. They could read something like this:

Flying south this year, and want your car?
I'll drive it there for you. Senior citizen
has _____ years driving experience. Why
not contact me for further information?

A real estate man in Montreal flies to Naples, Florida every fall. His car is driven there and the driver returns in the spring and brings the vehicle back. "This arrangement is much less expensive than renting a car," says the customer.

15

An Airport Valet Car Service Fills a Need

A new type of service which retirees have ventured into, and which is becoming very popular, is an airport valet service. You drive people to the airport and pick them up either at a designated time, or when they phone you. You drive them in their own car, and you either keep the car at your place, or return it to their home and pick it up when needed.

This service eliminates a lot of problems for the person using a standard valet service. It eliminates the problem of a person removing their bags from their car and then parking it. It also removes the necessity of carrying bags and walking to the car on returning. On cold days the car is warm, and there is no possibility of not getting the car started. Possible damage while parked is generally eliminated.

The charge made by the retiree can be the same or even lower than the airport parking charge, and offers the retiree a worthwhile profit. This is the type of service that builds a repeat customer service, so it can be very profitable.

Driving the Girls at Night

Another service performed by retirees is driving elderly ladies to social events in the evening. These ladies often have cars, but don't wish to drive at night. A group will chip in to pay the driver for his service. The retiree can easily build up a steady business for this service, and would, of course, use one of the women's cars. If it is a card party, or a night of shopping, the retiree can also play cards or shop.

16

Miss White and Her Little Restaurant

Miss White, while in her sixties, decided to start a small restaurant in the town where she lived. She converted a store that had been a restaurant previously, but the owner had moved away to a larger city. The only things he left behind were a Coke cooler and a ten-foot wooden counter. Fortunately the rent, about $250 a month, had been paid up-to-date.

There was another restaurant down the street, but this lady decided she could make a living from hers if she put her mind to it. There were various company signs, soft drinks, etc., on the front of the store left over from the prior restaurant days. She painted the place white and changed the name of the store to the "White House Restaurant."

She was unattached, and also had little money. She did, however, have an insurance policy which had paid-up dividends which were worth about $1,000. She had two choices open to get this money: she could take the policy to the bank and use it as collateral and thus get a loan at the prime rate, or borrow the money from the insurance company at a much lower interest rate as the policy had been in effect for over twenty-three years. She chose the latter and opened a business account at the bank.

She paid her first month's rent and was soon in touch with a wholesale restaurant supply house. Here she bought some used equipment. This consisted of a coffee urn, commercial toaster, a double hamburger grill, a bun warmer, refrigerator, and a counter with six stools. That along with a couple of tables each with four chairs just about filled the place. She found that distributors had various racks for display which they gave to her.

The bill for the used equipment came to $2,000. The suppliers make their money by having customers trade up to new equipment, so generally they are generous in their terms. In this case they took $500 down and spread the balance over a year at bank interest rates.

Miss White had always enjoyed cooking and realized that if she could offer tasty food to the villagers, she would be able to attract them. She believed that a specialty would be the thing that would make her place stand out.

Our new restauranteur had had some experience a few years earlier and it came into good use now. She knew that restaurant people usually figure the raw cost of food at about 25 to 30 percent of the selling price. Thus, if the ingredients in a sandwich cost thirty cents, the selling price would be about ninety cents.

Labor, utilities, and rent, the next big items, run about one-third of every dollar taken in. This leaves about 35 percent for interest on loans, equipment, insurance, and profit.

A specialty food that would make people remember Mrs. White's place was what was needed, and she recalled hearing about restaurants in larger cities offering their specialty at wholesale prices to other restaurants in outlying districts.

She decided to offer sandwiches made of a well-known smoked meat (brisket of beef). Each morning, or as was required, she would receive uncut smoked meat, fresh loaves of rye bread, and dill pickles. By now Miss White had a part-time waitress and the supplier of smoked meat had shown both women how to cut the beef and make the sandwiches.

Before long the sandwich sales had outstripped hot dogs and hamburgers by a wide margin, and total sales were running about $200 a day. Store hours had been 10 A.M. to 10 P.M. Then Miss White decided to offer breakfast, as salesmen passing through the town began requesting this service. So a breakfast special was offered, and this soon began to pay for itself. It was necessary to hire a full-time waitress. The restaurant had never been open on Sundays, but about a year after the place was first opened it became obvious that Sunday business could be very profitable. However, this would mean that the "boss" would have to work seven days a week.

She would shortly be eligible for her old-age pension, so she decided to sell.

She now had a thriving business with sales for a full year running around $100,000, not a big gross for a restaurant, but large enough to attract some prospective buyers. One of the real estate firms agreed to try and sell the business on a 4 percent commission basis. The price was set at $60,000. All equipment had been paid for. An offer of $55,000 was made with half cash down, the balance to be paid over five years without interest. This would give Miss White about $5,500 a year and work in very well with her social security.

She planned a trip to Europe, and after paying the agent's commission ($3,000) she would still have a healthy sum to invest if she wished.

So, even if you are ready for retirement or already have retired, think about the restaurant or food business. Everybody has to eat!

17

Preston Retiree Makes Money with Display Cards

"If you have the will, here is the way," says Alf McGlynn of Preston, Ontario.

For thirty-eight years Alf worked for the railway. Four years ago he retired. Prior to that time he had decided that "a man or woman coming up to the retirement years has to have some hobby or interest to keep mind and hands busy."

Having a little artistic ability and fascinated by the printed word, Alf decided to learn the business of making advertising placards or display cards. There were few if any places that would hire an apprentice for this trade, so the best method was to practise and also go to the library and obtain books on the subject.

Occasionally in the past, Alf had turned out a beautifully printed banner for some special event. He began to check into his new profession more closely. First he went to an art supply shop and purchased all the materials he would need. After two months of practise in calligraphy he was delighted with the professional look of his work. His customers probably wouldn't pay top dollar so they really didn't expect completely professional work, but certainly the display material he turned out would have to be "acceptable."

He started by visiting the retailers in the small city where he lived. He showed them samples and three gave him orders. Churches, schools, and other public institutions also began to call on him. Then he contacted merchants in nearby areas and picked up a few more accounts.

He says he is making a good second income and he has as much work as he can handle, and was never happier. He purposely keeps his sign business on a low-key basis because he likes to maintain it as a hobby and not a "busy" business.

If he was younger, says Alf, he would rent a suitable garage for a sign shop. It would have to be large enough to accommodate trucks for lettering. There is a great demand for applying pictorial effects to vans and pick-up trucks.

Now he has to turn down all types of sign work, and refers it to outside sign shops. "If this type of work appeals to you," says Alf, "check it out. If you're at all good at sign work you can always get orders and make money fast."

18

There's Money in Comic Books

*H*arold S. has been collecting comic books as a hobby for the last thirty years. He found that he devoted more room to them than to himself.

He phoned the local newspaper and told them about the thousands of comic books he had. They thought it was hot news and rushed a photographer over. A few days later a story came out showing Harold surrounded by his comic books. He was soon getting calls from all over the country from people who either had some comic books and wanted to add to their collections or wanted to buy a few just for nostalgia. He priced them from a couple of dollars up to ten dollars per copy depending on age, condition and rarity. The result was that he got rid of about half of his collection. He says he made money on the deal and now has room to move around his apartment.

19

Life Doesn't End at Seventy—
It Begins!

Gordon Green will soon be seventy-two, and he says he's the only person in Ormstown, P.Q. (not far from the New York border) who gets the old-age pension and the baby bonus. He's an example for all retirees who complain that there is nothing to do.

He operates a 200-acre farm. He does a live weekly radio show which is heard on over 100 stations across Quebec and Ontario at 7 A.M. He is also heard at least once a week on a noon-hour show. He writes articles, short stories, and books which are published regularly. He teaches English and journalism at an Indian Reserve school (he recently retired from a teaching position at a university and is very popular on the lecture circuit). He also does a weekly column for the *Toronto Star.*

"Keeping going, keeps me young," he says. "I feel sorry for people who don't like to work." Gordon can still do as much, if not more work than a half-dozen average younger people.

He's started all sorts of projects after the normal retirement age, such as doing a weekly column for a big city daily, breeding all manner of livestock on his farm, and has other accomplishments.

"I've only just begun," says Gordon!

20

Don't Neglect Your Old Company

When they give you that gold watch, pat you on the back and shake hands, don't walk away forever. There is an ever-increasing number of retirees who are returning on a part-time basis to their old company. Sometimes the job they get may be even more interesting and pay more money than the work they were doing before.

One man working in the office of a roofing company retired, and a few months later his firm introduced a credit union. This job would require half-days only. This man, after retiring, had returned to his old shop every few weeks to see the boys. On one such trip he learned about the credit union coming in and applied for this part-time job. He got it, and now along with his pension he is making more money than he ever made before and it keeps him out of the kitchen, much to the relief of his wife.

Six months after a woman left her job with an automotive supply parts company, the firm was sold. The new owners were desperately in need of information about all phases of the operation. Somebody mentioned Jessie. She had been there for forty years. She knew all the answers. Because she had kept in touch with what was happening with her old firm she got a call back. Now she is classified as a consultant. She works part-time but makes excellent money.

Normand F. worked for an insurance company in Montreal. He retired. When he was sixty-seven the insurance company put in a computerized system and he was asked to come in and spend a few hours a day cross-checking the names of clients. He was delighted to get this position which earned him enough money to take a three-month winter holiday in Florida.

Magazine publishers frequently call on their retired editors to come in and help, when producing special annual issues. Because of the experience these people have, they are far more efficient than any newcomer might be. Said one such retired person to me, "Now the company is paying me a pension and a salary. I can whip through the work faster than these young people and I get a real kick out of doing it."

Those in the know say "let your old company know that you are still around"; you are still able to do a good job, and you might be able to help them out of a lurch and also put some extra dollars in your pocket.

21

Desmond Kelly Got Ready Early for Retirement with Typewriters

*F*or most of his business life, Desmond Kelly was associated with the sale of typewriters. When he neared his sixtieth birthday, he was salesmanager for a divisional office of a large typewriter firm.

Retirement days weren't too far away, so Desmond decided to start doing something about it at once. He knew that there were three important departments in the operation of a successful typewriter operation. The first was sales, which he knew, and next was repairs of which he knew nothing. The third category was rentals which he knew wouldn't be a problem. He decided not to wait for official retirement but to get going at once. So he opened an office-showroom in his basement.

His son, Peter, began studying books on typewriter repairs and was soon able to handle this phase of the business.

Desmond knew that he could get at wholesale any make or model of typewriter he had orders for, so he was actually ahead of competitors who specialized in only one brand.

This typewriter man now has a great little business going. He has taken attractive showroom offices on the second floor of a conveniently located building. There are two full-time mechanics, plus his son, and a girl in the office.

Desmond Kelly doesn't worry about retirement. He's worked out his own program and his only regret is that he didn't start his business years ago.

22

Your "Old" Skills Are Worth Money

Bert Carr of Lachine, P.Q. is eighty-four. During his working years he was associated with the advertising agency business. He said to me that over the years he had built up a pretty good knowledge of the agency business so he let it be known that he was available as a consultant for promotion and advertising ideas and similar propositions. He started to get calls for advice, and he's still getting them. He doubts if any of his colleagues are still active in the business, but if they wanted to be he's sure they could stir up a lot of business. He finds that the new, younger crowd moving into the business often realizes that experience can often bring forth ideas that theoretical knowledge can't match.

Mr. Carr, who has been in two world wars, says that the man who has been active all his life who suddenly stops in his tracks at the age of sixty-five is asking for trouble. Slow down a little if you wish, he claims, but keep doing something.

23

Start a Mini-Dry-Cleaning Route

One very pleasant way of earning a second income without working too hard is to operate a dry cleaning route. You will require a vehicle for pick up and delivery, and if you have to buy a truck, a standard unit is best, jobber-salesmen (as they are called) told me. In several interviews, jobbers said that while the smaller vans are easier on gas, they don't have the height, and long dresses touch the floor. So, if buying a unit, make sure it has plenty of height. At the beginning your car will do, but once again you will have the height problem. You will need to put a pole or rod cross-ways on which you can hang the clothes.

A showcard fitted to the side windows is good advertising. This would carry the name of the cleaner doing your work, or you might want to use a name of your own choosing. However, if your name is unfamiliar, and the name of the cleaner is in the phone book, use the latter. Having customers use the company phone number is also good business.

An increasing number of dry cleaners offering delivery service prefer to have contractors look after this aspect of the business. Here's why: the jobber (contractor) is in business for himself. He pays all vehicle expenses including insurance. The cleaner makes no employee deductions such as pensions, insurance, medicare, workman's compensation, etc. This eliminates a lot of paperwork for the boss. In return you will get at least a 50 percent commission. You are responsible for any credit losses on your accounts. The cleaner is responsible for any damage claims. This should be spelled out on the bill you give the customers.

The wide-awake cleaner will supply you with "Call Cards." You hand these out to prospects in your territory (new peo-

81

ple moving in and those you do work for). On certain days you drive along chosen streets looking for cards in the windows. The cards should mention the days you are in a particular area. This information can be printed on the back of the card. On the front all that is required is a single large letter; the letter is the first letter of the name of the cleaner.

In most areas, a man's suit brings $5 to clean and press. It doesn't take too many garments to earn a good living.

You would have to decide, along with the cleaner, which territory would be yours. Phone calls for pickup from your area would be credited to you, but you normally would not get a commission on orders brought to the store (if there is one) by the customer. It is extremely important that work be of high quality, and delivery is made on the day promised. Deliveries to a certain district would be made on same day as pickups. Work picked up on Mondays is normally delivered on Wednesdays, and Wednesday's work is delivered on Fridays. There is no Saturday delivery or pickup. Old-timers in the business say don't offer to break your schedule—it will only mean more work and neglect of other customers.

Those in the business say keep away from shirts. At seventy-five to ninety cents for cleaning, you can't make any money. Many cleaners won't touch hats or certain special garments. As a contractor you can always have this work done elsewhere, but generally you are wise to not handle any items your own shop can't do.

If you don't want to work too hard, choose a small area. Your cleaner hopefully will do some general advertising which should help you, however, canvassing is considered to be the best way of getting business. Even calling once a week on prospects and old customers can build sales.

So if you don't want to work too hard, choose a small area and cultivate it thoroughly. Watch out for apartment buildings though. You may not be allowed to canvass them, but you might be able to make a deal with the janitor. He has dry cleaning, too!

24

How About a Little Dry Cleaning Plant?

*I*f you're not familiar with the dry cleaning business you may have visions of a big factory, and even bigger machines. At least that's the way it appeared to me when I was younger. But all that's changed now. The washers and dryers are hardly any larger than those found at home, and just about as simple to operate.

A retiree might start such a business, and spend his time taking orders (and money) if it was a busy operation, and most of them are today. Your main costs are a couple of employees, monthly payments on your machines, rent, and utilities. Your only material costs are the solvent used to wash the clothes. This runs $6 to $8 a gallon, and it's recycled so you can do a goodly number of garments with the same solution. You'll need small bottles of a few other chemicals for removing difficult spots, but apart from this, materials are minimal. And, unlike the old days, you don't have to deliver to get the business, so you can operate from a small store.

I know one retiree who has a dry cleaning store which is twelve feet wide and about fifty feet deep. He has a presser, who also does some "spotting"—looking for stains in clothes that require special attention. There is a woman at the front desk, and the owner works in every department depending on the need. He told me he takes in $500 a day.

The plant was in operation when this chap bought it, but the owner had let it run down. He wanted $35,000 but eventually sold it for $25,000. The new owner paid part down and part out of profits. He knew nothing about the business, but the female employee had been there fifteen years and she taught the boss the business in two weeks. You can always go to the firms that make dry cleaning equipment and they can assist you. In this case the cleaning machine was a Marten; it was about twenty years old but still doing a good job.

There are four basic pieces of equipment to a small plant. A washer, a boiler, a dryer, and a presser. A standard washer takes about thirty-five pounds of clothes and the wash cycle takes half an hour. Doing suits in an hour is no trick if you wish to offer fast service.

One equipment distributor told me that a new washer runs between $15,000 and $20,000, but you can pick up a used one for $5,000, and sometimes less. A new dryer can cost $10,000 but used ones can be purchased for half or less.

"Shopping centers are great places to set up shop. One cleaner told me that when he opens his store in the morning there are always three or four people waiting with clothes to be cleaned. They call for the work on their way home from the office.

An old trick worth trying if there is another cleaner nearby is to take in an item when the store opens. Then take in another just before it closes. Serial numbers on bills run consecutively, so you can tell how much business (orders) the place is doing and whether it is worth locating near that shop. Dry cleaning can be a busy, hectic business, so if you like work you'll love it. You can also hire a young person to run around, while you just supervise.

The Way It Used to Be . . .

The business today has changed. In the '30s if you wanted to open a dry cleaning store you were almost always a tailor who would probably make much of his money by repairing clothes. If you decided to personally open a little store you would go to a cleaning plant in the industrial section of town, and the boss would come out and say, "Okay, we'll do your work, a dollar a suit less 35 percent for you. Let me know when you want us to pick up. Good luck."

If you went directly to a manufacturer of cleaning equipment they would probably ask you what capacity machines you wanted, and when you wanted delivery.

The next phase happened about 1935-40 when the big chains got going. Isadore Paul of New York opened a couple of hundred stores there. Then, under the name of Paul, he came to Montreal and opened eighty-five stores. He admitted he couldn't even press a pair of pants. Soon an opportunity for mass low-priced cleaning developed. Companies which had operated plants and truck delivery service began opening chains of stores. With the coming of the war, many of them dropped their delivery service altogether. Then a new breed came along.

This was engineered by the equipment manufacturers. The old-time tailor who could do everything was replaced by the smart young college-educated chap with the briefcase and multicolored circulars. He was, in some instances, such as Marten, a franchise operation. Now you could get a turn-key operation: leased, equipped and ready to go.

There are still some franchise operations: Marten of Cincinnati, Ohio, is probably the best known. Equipment manufacturers will advise you, and install your equipment on an outright sales deal. They'll also offer training assistance to you or your staff.

One Canadian equipment distributor (most if not all equipment sold in Canada is made in the U.S.) told me that $75,000 to $100,000 is not an unusual sum to equip a ready-to-go store-plant. One thing about a dry cleaning plant, you can usually sell it at a profit once you get it going.

You can usually get in for a reasonable down payment for new equipment. Some people take a mortgage on their house. But the most sensible thing for a senior to do is take three months and look around. Call on cleaners—you'll find them friendly and talkative. And call on equipment manufacturers. Study their brochures, and examine their equipment.

On the following page are the names of some equipment manufacturers and distributors that specialize in working with small operators:

Calmek Equipment Ltd.
5653 Pare Street.,
Montreal, P.Q.
H4P 1S1

Maytag Commercial
Distributors:
10301 Ray Lawson
Ville d'Anjou, P.Q.
H1J 1L6

Stalwart Machinery &
Supplies, Inc.
1133 Sanford Street,
Winnipeg, Manitoba
R3E 3A1

G-NET Canada Ltd.
Distributor,
625 President Kennedy,
Suite 400
Montreal, P.Q.
H3A 1K2

Euroclean Canada Inc.
866 Langs Drive
Cambridge, Ont.
N3H 2N7

Maritime Equipment Ltd.
100 Royal Ave.
Sydney, Nova Scotia
B1P 4M3

In the U.S.—
American Permac, Inc.
200 Frank Road
Hicksville, N.Y. 11801

Milnor International
P.O. Box 400
Kenner, LA 70063

25

A Rental Uniform Service Fills a Need Everywhere

*H*ere is a service in demand which can be handled very well by senior citizens. Very simply, you supply gas stations and other firms with clean uniforms each week.

Let's say a gas station needs ten freshly laundered uniforms a week; you would have to purchase twenty, and probably arrange to have the name of the station (front or back) on each. On the back of the collar you would also have a tag with the name of the wearer.

You could arrange to have the customer pay for the uniforms, plus a regular weekly cleaning charge, or you could supply the uniforms and include a weekly charge to pay for the garments.

The cost could be spread over a year. As your capacity for laundering, or dry cleaning, increases, you could add more customers. If you didn't want to do the work with your own staff, you could farm it out on a wholesale price basis to a cleaner.

Some dry cleaners, for example, are strictly wholesale. They might have two or three dozen wholesale customers, some who have stores, or truck delivery, but they themselves have no individual customers.

A garment rental business requires a car or truck, and some starting capital. Some operators have started with as little as $2,000.

26

Parlour Parties Are Popular and Profitable

*I*t first started in the early Depression in mother's front parlour. And if you're in the retirement bracket, you'll no doubt remember those parties. Not the gramophone with the Rudy Vallee record parties, but the type where a hostess demonstrated such items as cosmetics, kitchenware, and so forth. Your mother probably got a free gift for inviting the girls to the party. She usually supplied coffee, too, and maybe even some of her homemade goodies. After all, with doughnuts selling at twenty cents a dozen, who could afford the luxury of store-bought cakes? As I recall, there was only one woman on our street who ever supplied the baker's products at such parties, and no wonder! Her husband was a bricklayer making a dollar an hour!

Today though, the home demonstration parties are bigger than ever. One of the best-known names is Tupperware, but there are jewelry parties, gifts, cosmetics, dresses, and various other products that lend themselves to parties.

The operating formula is very simple. The local agent for the sponsoring company suggests that you run a party. You will be expected to invite your friends, relatives, neighbors, and any other girls you happen to know. It's a sort of chain letter affair, or perhaps chain telephone is more accurate.

The lady running the show, which could be you, arrives about 7.30 P.M., if it is going to be an evening affair, or about 1.30 if it is to be held in the afternoon. Senior citizens often prefer daytime parties.

The hostess running the show usually brings a stock of the products to be sold. If business is good there may be a shortage of certain items which are delivered later, but preferably paid for then.

Women tell me that they can clear $15 to $50 a party, and three or four parties a week are not unusual. Some ladies who run these parties often prefer to take things a little easier, and find that two parties a week are sufficient.

The success of the business depends on the ability of the hostess to have a constant supply of ladies who will hold a party in their homes. Usually one person is singled out for this honor at each party. All you need do is approach one of the girls who seems to be a bit of an extrovert and say, "Oh, Gertrude wouldn't you like to hold one of our parties in your home? How about next Thursday at eight?"

You'll usually get an "okay" from someone. You can offer the person a gift for her trouble, and even something to cover the coffee cost.

Once you get started on your own, you'll probably love it, and financially you can do very well. If you're stuck for companies offering party products, look in the "classifieds" of the newspaper under "money-making opportunities," or "sales people wanted."

Firms in party planning merchandising have offices throughout the U.S. and in many parts of Canada. Here are the names and addresses of some of the firms:

Beeline Fashions
Beeline Dr.
Bensenville, Il.
60108

Tupperware
Orlando, Fla.
32802

Home Interior and Gifts
4550 Spring Valley Road
Dallas, Texas
75240

Fashion Two Twenty
151 Skyway Ave.
Rexdale, Ont.
M9W 4Z5

Mary Kay Cosmetics
5600 Ambler Dr.
Mississauga, Ont.
L4W 2K9
Phone: 624-5600

Aloe-Mist Inc.
Arlington, Texas
76011

Princess House
455 Somerset Dr., N.
Dighton, Mass.
02764
(decorative home accessories)

Shaklee Corporation
1900 Powell St.
Emeryville, Calif.
94608
(nutritional supplements and foods, personal care and household products)

Stanhome Inc.
140 Ann St.
London, Ont.
N6A 1R3

Coppercraft
Kitchener, Ont.

Complexe le Baron
6020 Jean Talon Est.
No. 610
St. Leonard, P.Q.
H1S 3B1

Sarah Coventry Jewelry
Newark, N.J.
14593

Aubrey McDonald Ltd.
Galaxie Blvd.
Rexdale, Ont.
(jewelry)

Many firms, not normally known as party planning operators, allow their representatives to sell any way they wish. And because house parties have become so popular, many direct sales firms (companies which don't normally go through stores) are advising and assisting representatives who wish to sell through parties. Two of these firms are Watkins and Rawleighs, names which will be household words to retirees and others. There wasn't a farm house in the west (or the east too) who didn't know the Watkins or Rawleigh man.

Rawleighs' head offices are located in Winnipeg, Manitoba, and at 354 Isabey Street in Montreal. Watkins' head office is at 5640 Louis Hebert St., Montreal.

A Watkins manager told me that one representative in the eastern U.S. makes $3,000 a month, and does no sales work.

He has some twenty agents working for him, and because of his large buying power he is able to earn big discounts and sell to agents at probably the same price they would pay if buying directly.

27

Clip Newspaper Items for Profit

You've probably seen this heading ·in ads in publications, and possibly even sent for the free literature. You may have even gone further and sent the $6 to $10 asked by different mail order operators for their booklet which tells how to get into the business.

I'm a very curious person. I send for all kinds of booklets, free and otherwise, so I know about most of the newspaper clipping operations. They are perfectly legitimate, and after you've read this chapter you might even want to start a press clipping business, or make even more money by telling other people how to do it. Most mail order dealers put out a twelve to twenty-page "how to" guide. It costs them about sixty cents to print and they sell it for $6 or $7. The postage probably costs thirty-five cents. But these people are selling information and ideas.

These mail order operators always give a money-back guarantee on the guide because not more than one percent of buyers ever asks for their money back. Most readers feel that maybe someday they'll be able to make use of the information.

The second interesting fact is that not even one percent of people who buy a booklet on a given subject ever act on the booklet's advice or direction.

The ads say you will make a fortune. You won't, but you can make some money without spending very much, and you don't have to go out of the house.

Here's how the newspaper clipping business works. Magazines of all kinds, particularly business magazines (trade journals) carry news items. If you skimmed through a few of the more than 5,000 business publications in North America, you would find all sorts of news items. In a grocery magazine you might find something like this: "Fire Causes $50,000 Damage in Brown's Supermarket."

"Winnipeg: George Brown, owner of Brown's Supermarket, reports that his store was completely gutted by fire in early November. The fire was said to have been started by an overheated furnace.

"The business was started eighty years ago by the grandfather of the present owner who reports he is covered by insurance, and that rebuilding will start at once."

This particular publication might carry a couple of dozen items a month pertaining to the grocery business. Hardware publications will carry items pertaining to that business, and so on.

These items have to come from somewhere, and they do— often from retirees who get $3 to $10 and sometimes more per item. All you need is a sharp pair of scissors, one or two daily newspapers, and a weekly paper published locally. In fact, you might be better off with two or three weeklies, unless the daily is strong on local news.

Very simply, you clip the item, mention the date and the paper, and send the clipping to a magazine in that business. If you are near a photocopying machine you may want to send the item (copy) to another magazine in the same business. Most of these papers rewrite these items anyway, and they don't usually give credit lines.

Your library has magazine directories, and there are some mentioned elsewhere in this book. Writer's directories are useless for this task as they don't carry a complete list of publications.

Editors will get to know you, and look forward to your material. If you're ambitious, you can touch up such items by adding a little additional information. In the case mentioned, you would phone Brown. Then you can get yourself a by-line and a bigger check. Last week I got a small check, $38, for a six-inch item I clipped from the *Montreal Gazette*, and rewrote. Total time involved, fifteen minutes.

You cannot learn the press clipping business overnight: you must study the business magazines and newspapers. You won't sell everything you send out, but your record will improve as you go along. Sometimes you will come across news items which haven't yet, or may not, appear in the newspaper. Then you have a minor scoop.

If you wish to rewrite or touch up an item, you don't even have to include the clipping. If you are going to make money, production is important. By the way, use rubber cement to paste your items on standard letterhead sheets. It always pays to use a printed letterhead advertising your name and address, and the words "Press Clipping Service" or something similar.

I have to tell you there are some commercial companies in the business which offer the same service as you will be offering, except for a couple of differences. Not all magazines get the commercial services. They charge a monthly rate, plus so much a clipping. And, they aren't anywhere near as fast as you would be. Walk into a press clipping office and you may find a number of girls clipping away with stacks of newspapers in front of them, some dailies a couple of weeks old. Usually one girl goes through the papers and writes a number on an item. Thus a hardware publication customer is No. 738. All hardware items the checker comes across get this number. It is eventually cut out, passed to the shipper who finds the name and address to which this number belongs, and mails it out.

You would be offering a much more personal service which fills a real need. Magazines can't afford to have reporters in every area. I know one retiree who averages $150 a month sending out clippings. She specializes in sending out items to three business publications, and gets dailies from two cities.

Consumer magazines seldom take clippings unless they are of general news value. Such publications are sold on newsstands and by subscription. Moreover, these publications usually want an in-depth report which means you have to research and write. I saw a newspaper item about a school for expectant fathers which taught them how to diaper babies, and otherwise care for them. The school was in Detroit. I wrote for a photo and further facts and this became a 1,000-word feature for a major magazine.

So there you are. There's the whole course on the newspaper clipping business, and I hope you do well with it.

28

Profits on the Highways

Thomas N. got fed up with his job so he quit and started a trucking company. Sounds like big business? He told me that his total investment was well under $1,000.

How did he do it? Simple, he says. First he chose a name, then he became limited. The service he offered was to industry and it was the pickup and delivery of just about anything a company wanted to ship. He had studied rates, tariffs, etc., and so he knew what the going prices were for such work.

He knew that transport vehicles cost tens of thousands of dollars, so rather than get into that category he decided to contact a half-dozen different trucking companies. He found that some firms, because of the type of vehicles they had, specialized in certain kinds of delivery. He contacted these firms and told them that he would like them to handle his hauling contracts on a 10 percent commission basis. A few of the trucking firms were working day and night and didn't want any more business, but there were some who were interested.

Thomas then had letterheads printed, made out a list of prospective companies in a given area, called representatives of those companies, and had an outside stenographer type letters announcing his service. At one point in his life, Thomas, who is about sixty years of age, had worked for a rubber firm who had used outside transports. He realized that there are fewer and fewer firms operating their own vehicles; they either utilize the services of a leasing system, or employ outside carriers. Whichever methods they use there are always times when there is a need for additional services.

Thomas waited for his letters to be received. Next, he made an appointment and called on this or that particular manager. One company had some instant business, while others said they would let him know. All these firms wanted was service at a standard price. He was able to assure them that he could guarantee both. He knew that his prices were in line and because he had chosen reliable carriers, he had no fears regarding service. Of course he didn't have to worry about the licensing of vehicles, insurance, paying drivers' salaries, unions, or any other problems. He was merely a man working on commission.

The carriers liked his idea because they in turn had no obligation to him such as salary, holidays, and tax deductions. Thomas was in business for himself.

Thomas had invoices printed bearing his company name, such as YZ Transport Company. He would collect and then reimburse the trucking firm less his 10 percent commission. His invoice would state which carrier picked up the shipment. In a few cases the trucking company did their own invoicing and paid Thomas his commission in thirty days.

If Thomas went out of town, he arranged to have someone check with his answering service and farm out any orders. If one carrier was too busy to make the pickup when the customer wanted it, then a second transport firm was called. Thomas's main selling point was service and he made sure he gave it.

"Got a thousand trucks on the road," he boasted to me, "and my expenses are about $60 a month. It's the kind of service that's always in demand no matter where you live. And there is no physical work involved, so I'll probably keep right on going till I'm a hundred."

He told me that within a year he was making a far better income than he ever made as a salaried man.

29

A Pool Service Could be Popular

There are many services in demand that can be supplied by the retiree and people in his employ.

I heard of one senior who has a pool cleaning service. He employs a couple of young chaps to do the work. This retiree signs up customers for the season, just as some individuals offer snow removal, or a lawn service. You can let your grass grow for an extra week or so, but if you own a pool (above or below ground), it has to be attended to regularly.

When dad comes home from the office he's ready to enjoy a swim, but he doesn't relish the idea of cleaning the pool. And, of course, the kids have other things to do. So such a service does have appeal.

You would have to supply chemicals, probably cleaning equipment, and whatever else is called for. You might need a light truck or station wagon. All this can be charged off as expenses when you report your additional income.

What your charge should be depends on the frequency of service and length of time spent at each pool. If you paid an employee $4 an hour, for example, you would have to charge at least $12 an hour to cover your costs and profit.

A little survey, carried out either by phone or by personal visits, would give you a clue as to whether or not there was a need for such a service. Your next step is to figure out how many customers you need to make such a service viable.

30

Day-Old Bread Stores Offer Profit Opportunity

*I*t seems that many senior citizens have time to get around and see things. In your travelling, have you noticed the increase in day-old bread stores? The reason, I suppose, is that bread, like other products, is constantly going up in price.

Not all people who buy their bread and baked goods at these places are poor. Some people prefer bread that isn't too fresh.

In the old days, say twenty-five years ago, bakeries generally sold their "stale" at the back door and the buyers were poor. Today, however, while a few bakeries sell their returns from the supermarkets at the bakery, most of these products are sold from retail shops.

If there isn't this type of service in your area, you might care to consider opening one. You would get your baked goods from the bakery which would probably be pleased to sell them to you. Your discount would have to include the reduced price you would have to sell the product for, plus your own discount. This would have to cover your store rent, utilities, and possibly at least one clerk.

In some cities where you have a number of big bakeries you will find at least one "stale" shop for each bakery.

Maybe one day some smart operator will open a "stale stale" shop, and sell the bread not sold by the one-day-old stores.

The changing economy, and changing life-styles, make for all sorts of new ventures, and this often spells opportunity for people of all ages who keep on the lookout.

31

Pottery and Ceramics Offer Many Advantages

Pottery is one of the oldest of the known arts. It offers an opportunity for men and women to develop their creative skills. You will, however, not become an expert overnight.

Said one lady, "I bought some supplies and a potter's wheel and took some lessons, but didn't seem to be creating anything of which to be really proud. Then one day it happened. I knew that I had mastered the art, and was turning out work I could be proud of."

She now produces about twenty pieces a week in her home, most of which are handled by stores. With the firing and finishing, it takes about two weeks to finish a piece.

She says, "Whenever I finish a piece of pottery it is like opening a Christmas gift. I am never sure of exactly what I have. It is an interesting hobby for retirees. All you need is a little patience at first. And don't stick to turning out the same type of work all the time. Visit places where pottery is on display, so that you can see what is being produced. This way you will be able to develop a style of your own, and if people like your work, you can do well financially, too."

NOTE: In many areas there are shops which have complete equipment where craftspeople can produce pottery and ceramics. This could be on a rental basis. These places frequently teach the trade, and will sell the products produced.

32

Flea Markets and Garage Sales Are Valuable Places

*I*f your interest is antiques, don't overlook flea markets and garage sales. One elderly couple reported that they spend a lot of their free time attending such events in search of glassware of which they are serious collectors.

People who offer antiques to the public are generally not experts in all or any of the items they want to get rid of. So whatever your interest is, you may find a small fortune at such places.

I acquired an old-fashioned sofa and six chairs as part of the furnishings of a house I bought. I decided to have the house painted as I wanted to resell it. I sent the furniture off to a gallery on a percentage deal if sold. My wife wanted to keep one of the chairs of the set. The others went off and eventually I received $25 for the set. A year later a person knowledgeable in antique furniture offered me $75 for the single chair. He was able to tell me the age, style, and other information on it. The smart person who bought the set no doubt made a thousand dollars on my ignorance. But we can't be experts on everything, so if you're a collector or restore items for resale you could discover a lot of bargains in flea markets and garage sales.

There is now a Canadian magazine called *Collectibles* which proves that the business is really getting big. The quarterly is published by Southam Publishing, 1450 Don Mills Road, Don Mills, Ontario M3B 2X7 (416-445-6641). It is available at newsstands at $2.50 a copy, or $9 a year. A typical issue runs eighty pages and its editorial content covers glassware, pottery, porcelain, other types of antiques, personalities, and other information of interest to collectors.

33

Refurbishing Antique Cars

A senior I know said he had always liked old cars and had recently begun refurbishing antique models for hobbyists. This gentleman began by first making contacts through garages as to sources of supply for old body parts, tires, and so on. In some cases the parts would have to be made. A typical customer might be a person who bought a 1922 Chevrolet which needed a new fender, a tire or two, some upholstery repairs, and a paint job. A little work would probably be needed on the motor.

A repair job like this requires time and a lot of loving care. This person said he enjoyed his "hobby" and that his customers didn't mind paying a good price to have their "baby" refinished. He also said there was no lack of work, and garages supplied him with many leads as they had no time for this custom-repair business.

34

Pet Sitting Has Many Advantages

We are in a changing world, and services that weren't even thought of when we were young are quite the thing today.

In the old days, if you had a pet dog, cat, or bird, you might leave them with a friend or neighbor. People still do that, but with the big movement to apartments and townhouses, this practice is not always feasible.

There are senior citizens who will call at a person's home when the owner is away, and feed the pet, exercise it if necessary, and at the same time check on the premises. This can be a daily or twice-daily service, depending on what the client wants. Some seniors charge $20 or $25 a week, sometimes more, depending on what is required. Certainly for a person to go on holiday for a couple of weeks it is well worthwhile paying $50 for the peace of mind of knowing that Fido will be in good care, and the house is being checked against water leaks, and other possible problems.

Don't be bashful. Let it be known that you are offering this service. I heard of a girl who quit her regular job after starting this service, because it proved so popular and profitable.

A similar service that retirees can offer is to check on unoccupied houses for real estate firms which are trying to sell them. Sometimes this includes arranging to have the grass and hedge trimmed, snow removed, and otherwise have the place looking presentable if a prospective buyer shows up.

This is usually a weekly service with the rate being dependent on work required and distance between properties.

35

There's Always a Demand for Small-Office Space

A woman I know rents the entire sixth floor of an office building. It is not a large building and it is not new, but it is certainly adequate for the service which she offers.

What she has done is arranged the office into a series of cubicles using partitions which are about five feet high. There are two sizes of offices ranging from six feet by eight feet to double this size. Rents range from $110 to $150 per month including telephone service. This woman has two main lines in her office, and calls go through her. However, some of the people renting space do have their own telephone.

This woman also offers a stenographic service and takes calls for her tenants when they are out. Many of the tenants are manufacturers' agents, salesmen, insurance people, and others who are in and out of the office all day.

She rents the entire floor at a flat rate, and finds that there is never a shortage of tenants. In fact, she usually has a waiting list. She is able to make an excellent income and has been operating for ten years.

To start such a business, the first thing you need is space. You would have to check buildings with to-let signs, enquire from real estate brokers what they might have, and look for possible sources. Sometimes empty church halls, or warehouse space is available. At least 2,000 square feet is necessary if you are to make any money.

You would have to check carefully on heating, washroom facilities, and elevator service if the space you are renting is above two floors. Obviously, you would check to see if building taxes are included in your rent. Some owners want escalator clauses so when fuel and municipal taxes go up you would be required to pay a percentage.

As for local business taxes, each business renting from you should pay his own directly to the city. Your operation would be similar in some respects to operating a shopping mall, though few if any of your tenants would likely be in the retail trade. Classified advertising might be used to find you the quarters you want, and also the tenants to fill these quarters.

36

Classified Ads often Hold Gold

One senior says he averages $100 a week by reselling bargains he finds in the classified pages. He also listens to a radio program which has a swap-shop show. There are not many of these around but if you can find one it could be worth big money to you.

One lady heard a shortwave radio being advertised for $35 on a radio program. She phoned the seller and that evening bought the set. The next day she put her offer on the radio (same show) and asked $65 and she got her price.

Radio shows offering to announce classified items usually give the price and the phone number of the seller. You would phone the person advertising the item and either pay the asking price or make an offer. Then you in turn might offer the item on the next radio show, or in your local classified newspaper column, adding a certain amount for your trouble. You would have to buy at a good price in order to make a profit.

One man said he recently heard on a radio program that a fur coat was available for $125. He offered the lady $100 cash, she took it, and in a couple of days he had sold the coat for $175.

If you have no radio program in your area with free classified offers, then you might look through the newspaper classified column for bargains. People are very often in a hurry to get rid of something and don't mind taking a lower price for fast cash.

37

The John Stuart Story

John Stuart of Toronto, now in his late seventies, is still operating a business, Stuart House International, which started off as a kitchen table operation.

John was a salesman making $25 a week for a food firm in Winnipeg, and travelled all the way to British Columbia. One cold December day he returned to the office, sat down at a desk and began making out a sales report. John was about thirty at the time. "One day," he said to no one in particular, "I'm going to go in business for myself. That's where the money is!"

A clerk at a nearby desk started to laugh. "Every time you come back from a sales trip we hear that story. But never any action."

"I'm serious this time," said John. He put a sheet of paper in the typewriter, put his two typing fingers to work, and showed the result to the clerk. "See?"

"Bet you haven't got enough nerve to show that to the boss."

With that Stuart got up and walked into the boss's office and laid the note on his desk.

He read it and looked at John. He liked his Scottish employee who had done well during the two years he had been with the firm. "I could give you $30 a week if you'd consider staying."

But having made his decision, John, "the bonnie Scotsman," as he was called, was adamant. So he left then and there.

The year was 1933. Jobs were scarce, and worse still John had few assets. He sat down at the kitchen table with his wife and began figuring what he owned. There was a 1931

Ford two-seater that had cost $600 new. That was paid for but he couldn't sell it—he'd need it to get around. There was this week's pay of $25, but that would go for family needs. Then John went to a drawer and pulled out an insurance policy. It had a cash surrender value of $75. This would be his starting capital.

He told me years later, when my wife and I were guests in his $300,000 home in Florida, that he has since started many businesses—food canning, fish processing and foil wrap—but this was his first and thus most important. "I felt," he said, "that if I didn't start then, I'd never begin."

At that time a large food distributor was handling the Smith Brothers cough candy line across Canada. The product was made in Poughkeepsie, N.Y. Within a week, John had decided to become a food broker selling at wholesale to grocers, druggists, and other stores. And now he was on the night train for Poughkeepsie. He had to start with a product, so why not cough drops?

He had written a brief note to the brothers, whom he didn't know, mentioning that he'd be coming to see them shortly. When John arrived at the Smith Brothers' house he had no bag. He'd slept in his seat to save money. But he did have his well-worn briefcase under his arm.

Once introduced, his pitch was simple. He explained that while he realized that the food broker handling their line in Canada was doing a great job in Winnipeg and east, he believed sales were kind of slow out west. "I know that territory. I was born out there. I know the retailers. Transportation from Toronto out west is slow. It sometimes takes weeks to get one of your shipments to Calgary. I'll load my vehicle with your cough drops and deliver as I go. I'll triple sales in no time!"

John told me that the two brothers in their black suits and beards suggested that Stuart stay and have lunch with them. They were noncommital, but they liked daring enterprise. Hadn't they arrived in Poughkeepsie in the 1800s with virtually no money, and started a cough candy business that was to become a household word?

John was full of enthusiasm. All through the meal he told them how he would sell carloads of their product. He even

had a note of reference from his previous employer saying
what a good salesman he was.

The brothers didn't say much. "I didn't know if I was making any headway or not," he said later.

Then one of them pulled out a very large gold watch from
his vest pocket, looked at it and said, "Well, if you're going
to sell our candies in Canada you'll have to hurry. Your train
leaves in twenty minutes."

"You mean you're going to give me your line?" asked John.

"Just in the west," said the brothers. "We'll see how you
do. It will be C.O.D. of course."

"Of course," repeated John.

He caught his train and as he seated himself he wondered
if he would have enough cash left to pay the C.O.D. charge.
No one had thought to bring up the subject of the size of
the shipment.

The most important thing, decided John, was that he had
been successful in his first business venture. Now he was a
food broker on his own.

I guess in those days railway shipments travelled faster
than they do today because John said that about five days
after he got home he was sitting in his flat and the telephone
rang. It was the station agent. "We've a C.O.D. shipment here
for you."

"Wonderful," answered John fingering the balance of his
$75 in his pocket. "How much is it?"

"It's $10,000," replied the agent. "I can hold it for a couple
of days and then there is a storage charge."

John hung up the phone. It had to be a big shipment if it
came to $10,000. And that was wholesale. He couldn't figure
on the spur of the moment exactly how many packages there
would be. Maybe he'd been too enthusiastic with the Smith
Brothers. If they'd have sent him $500 worth of cough candy
... Even that would have been difficult to clear.

Still, Stuart had faith in his sales ability. But he had to
think fast. He couldn't even get any stock out of the railway
to sell it. It was all or nothing.

He couldn't go to the bank— he wouldn't mind paying the
interest rate it was charging, which was around 5 percent,
but he had no collateral for a loan. Then he had an idea! He

had a friend in the medical business who had money. He would use the cough candies as collateral! At retail they were worth much more than $10,000. Both his profit and the retailers' had to be added to that figure.

With all his enthusiasm back, John approached his friend with his deal. He offered to pay him for the use of the money which he hoped wouldn't be for long. The friend agreed to the deal and the shipment was out of hock. John said you could hardly get into his house for cough drops.

The Smith Brothers had recently come out with a menthol cough drop in addition to their well-known black one. So John got the idea of doing something to push the line. With every two cartons of black cough drops a store bought, they'd get a certain number of menthol packages free. And next morning he was off with his two-seater and trunk loaded with cough candies.

It seems that while drug stores had handled that line for years, no other types of merchants, grocery and general stores had ever been approached. The "free" offer turned out to be a winner. Most stores ordered, and within four or five weeks not only were the cough candies all gone, but an even larger order was placed. Stuart soon had all of Canada for the line, and had added George Washington Coffee, Edgeworth Pipe Tobacco, and some other lines.

His next step was to buy a building at 7 Duke Street, Toronto. It was an attractive building, four stories high. In order to raise the down payment he decided to rent the two upper floors at a reduced rate if the firms (one was a book club) would pay a couple of years' rent in advance. On the basis of the reduction they agreed to the deal. A third tenant's rent paid current costs for the building, and John had his own space without charge.

Soon he had twenty-five salesmen on the road and branch offices in principal cities. He added other lines, went public, but was still very active, along with his son. The last time I talked with him he said, "Why retire? It's more fun working!"

I mention the "Stuart Saga," as I like to call it, so that no one with an idea need be deterred by a shortage of money when starting a business. There's always an answer.

38

Nostalgia Is a Popular Theme

Small, old-fashioned shops are in vogue. Maybe the Walt Disney establishments have had something to do with it. If you have seen their "old-time shops" in California or Florida, you will have noticed how popular they are.

Retail stores patterned after the "early days" are coming into vogue everywhere. In Maui, Hawaii, every store has to follow the tradition of the pioneer shops. Many of the stores serving the public today haven't changed over the past century. You'll even find the cracker barrel and coffee grinders with the handle you turn for grinding.

In St. Anne de Bellevue, P.Q., there is an old-time general store which still uses wires strung across the ceiling that carries metal cash cups to the cashier's cage. The little metal money containers create a clicking and humming as they crisscross the ceiling.

There might be an opportunity in your town for an old-fashioned shop. A visit to either Disney location would give you many ideas. The most popular items are food.

You would need a revolving ceiling fan, and a Tiffany lamp or two. It would also help to have long wooden counters, a wall telephone, an old scale and a hand-operated cash register. These things will all help to create an "old-fashioned" atmosphere. And, of course, all your help should be dressed in costumes of the day.

Restaurants on Old Trams
The love of things nostalgic has probably reached its zenith in Melbourne, Australia. An ancient street car has been changed into a restaurant. However, this is not your typical trolley

111

car serving hamburgers and stationed on a vacant lot, which is not uncommon.

In this case the car is complete with its plush seats and other accoutrements of an earlier year. Moreover, the car is constantly moving with regular traffic and standard street cars.

The car is independently owned, seats thirty-six people, and dinner, including fine wines, costs $55. There are two dinner, and two lunch trips, and the length of travel time per meal is ninety minutes.

Is it popular? It certainly is. The service started toward the end of 1982, and almost immediately there was a reservation list extending over the next three months.

There is a complete galley on the car, though some of the foods such as roasts are precooked; there are wine stewards, and the tables are set with fine linen and china.

On the subject of memorabilia and dining places, one thinks of Ed's Warehouse on King Street, Toronto. There are two such restaurants, barely a block apart, under the same ownership. Each is reminiscent of an earlier day with its hanging lamps, antique furniture, and scores of other items which were so popular at the turn of the century and earlier.

If you have any product or service with which the "old days" can be associated, then maybe you can cash in on this theme.

Joe E. McDougall is a Canadian writer who writes about how things were when he was a boy. He retired fifteen years ago from an ad agency where, as he says, "he looked after everything except cleaning out the baskets."

"I thought I would tackle writing," Joe told me, "and what better theme than life in the old days."

His work has appeared in various papers and he recently (1982) had two by-lines in one issue of *Reader's Digest.* Says Joe, "We're just as smart as we were fifty years ago, but it takes us a little longer."

39

Rug Shampooing Service Makes Money for Retiring Teacher

A school teacher getting close to retirement invested $900 in a rug cleaning machine. He rents it out with the help of a classified ad and charges $30 a day. He says he's all set for his retirement.

His wife takes calls during the day, and when she goes out, she puts the phone on an automatic answering service.

This chap, who is fifty-nine, delivers his rug shampooer after his school day is finished. He includes enough cleaning fluid for an area about twelve feet square and sells additional solvent when the customer explains how big an area he or she intends to clean. There is an excellent profit in the cleaning liquid.

Although the supermarkets offer washing machine service, most of them don't deliver. Also the personal touch is quite effective as he tells you how to use the machine, and what to do for best results. Most customers rent the machine regularly, so there is a lot of repeat business.

He averages about $450 a month, clear. When he retires he intends to buy three more machines. He will earn a 25 percent discount by ordering three units. He says that he may employ a high school student to help him with deliveries.

His rug shampoo system is as good as any available. His prices are about 10 percent lower than retail stores. There is a definite need for this type of service because many people do not have the means available to transport one of these machines.

40

How to Plan Club Travel Tours

*I*f you like to travel, you might be interested in running club travel tours. It's exciting, can be very profitable, and you should get your own tours free.

I interviewed two travel agents and here is what I learned. First, either tie in with a group and use its name, or form your own club of which you would be president. This could be a gardening club, retiree club, or other special-interest group. At this point the club would not have to be in operation, but anyone taking your tour would automatically belong to your club.

Next, you would choose the area for your first tour. Let us say you are familiar with Jamaica, then this might be your destination. You would either go there and arrange hotel accommodation, dates, transfers, meals—MAP, modified American plan, which is breakfast and dinner—various sightseeing tours, or if possible, do the arranging from your home base. If the regular hotel rate was $50 a day, double, MAP, and you expected a group of thirty-five, the hotel might reduce the rate to $30 or $35 (per person). The hotel would also normally give you, as tour director, free accommodation and meals, double.

Your hotel people would ask for a deposit which would run 10 to 25 percent, the balance to be paid on checking out. As you sign people up for your tour you would ask them for a down payment. This could be $100 to $200 to show that they were serious. The balance would be payable thirty days before date of departure.

Your next step would be to go to an airline and explain that you wished to book thirty-five seats to Montego Bay, Jamaica. They would advise you dates available and what the cost would be by charter. With every fifteen seats they would offer you one free seat. You would tell them of your proposed package tour and they would give you a special rate. The reservation would have to be made well in advance of actual flying date (six weeks is normal). The airline would also ask for a deposit, with the balance before departure date, probably half. However, as you would have received full payment from your clients well in advance of departure, you would have little need to spend very much, if any, of your own money. For your work you would add at least 15 to 20 percent of tickets sold as your profit. Your clients would probably be saving at least a third over what they would pay if they went on an individual basis. They would save on air fare, hotel, special tours, transfers, and meals. The advantage of two meals a day means that your group would not have to return to the hotel for lunch.

You could not, say my sources of information, advertise to the general public as you would then not be considered a private, non-profit club, and would be obliged to be bonded and licensed, all of which is expensive and time consuming. However, as the operator of a club (the word travel normally does not appear in the name), you could send circulars to other groups similar to yours. This could be a camera club, artists' group, church group, etc.

If your name was John Smith, you might send out a circular to garden clubs which might read in part: "You have all heard of the wonderful horticultural activities in Jamaica. My gardening club, the John Smith Flower Club, is arranging a two-week all-inclusive trip to Jamaica at a price that will save you at least $200 over the single cost rate.

"I will be holding a showing on date ----- at -----. There will be movies of what you will actually see, a fashion show of island costumes, and coffee. Plus, of course, full information on the trip which is scheduled for ---. Why not decide now to attend this event and have an enjoyable evening. There is no obligation."

NOTE: You could place your tours through a travel agency and share the commission. This might be worth considering at the beginning until you have learned something about the fascinating world of travel.

I mentioned thirty-five members, but you could make this any number you wish. Airlines have a special charter division where group tours are welcomed. They will probably be able to give you advice, and copies of various brochures similar to yours.

When such tours are put out by travel wholesalers, who work with agents, their material is likely to be very colorful and expensive, as they are considered commercial operations. Because your tours would be considered private affairs, your printed material could be inexpensive.

There are also travel clubs which have monthly meetings, show movies, and hold lectures that you may wish to join.

41

A Fish Pond Can Be Profitable

*I*nterest is growing among people who have some vacant land—the possibility of raising trout for profit.

This is a big business, and an extremely helpful organization for anyone thinking of embarking on such a project is the Ontario Trout Farmers' Association, at R.R. 1, Campbellcroft, Ontario. This association has a membership of thirty trout farmers who supply stock to people with ponds. A list of members is available from the association. The association says that most ponds have a surface area of from one-quarter to two acres. Of course, ponds can be larger but they would require more work.

Ponds without constant inflow and outflow of water should be at least fifteen feet in depth over as large an area as possible. Ponds with water movement need only to be half this depth, though some deeper areas are recommended.

In the matter of what are the best species, the Ontario Trout Farmers' Association suggests native Brook (Speckled) Trout or Rainbow. These fish are popular with fishermen and make excellent eating. As for water temperature, trout can live in water just above freezing and up to eighty degrees Fahrenheit (27°C).

How many fish you should put in your pond will depend on the size of the pond, type of land, food, and other factors that will have to be decided before you go ahead. Fish are available as fingerlings, yearlings, or even older. In some cases 10,000 fry are recommended, or 1,000 advanced fry or 500 fingerlings or 300 yearlings per surface acre.

Established ponds with a planned stocking program can look forward to a continuous yield of large, healthy fish. Very

117

often a pond will supply enough food for its trout population
without the need of any artificial feeding.

Full details on how you can get started, sources of supply
of stock and prices can be obtained from the Ontario Trout
Farmers' Association.

42

Small Concession Departments Are Becoming Very Popular

There seems to be an increasing trend toward concession departments in various types of retail outlets.

I have found, for example, that in some of the largest F.W. Woolworth stores there are concessions operating. In Waikiki, where one of the largest and most beautiful Woolworth stores is to be found, there are five concessions owned and operated by women. The items offered were generally of the type purchased by tourists: novelties, postcards, scarves, and souvenirs.

Many large department stores operate the camera, jewelry, optical and hearing aid, hairdressing, and drugstore departments on a concession basis.

The idea is even growing in small towns where there are stores with some free space. In one town, a hardware store rents a space eight feet by twelve feet to a man who uses it to promote photo processing and the sale of cameras. In this case a flat monthly rental fee of $100 is charged. In larger stores the rent is often based on a percentage of sales. The management can determine this by a daily check of sales which go through the cash register.

In some instances a person may operate a number of concessions.

The Benefits of the Concession
The main values of a concession are you don't have to shop around for a retail store, you have no decorating problems, there are usually no licences as the main store pays this, and you don't have to worry about heating, insurance, or possibly any special advertising, as you would be drawing

119

on the traffic entering the store. In other words, you would
have a ready-made clientele.

Moreover, the store can often benefit from your department. It won't have to stock the merchandise, and staff it.
So if a retailer does have some free space, it could earn for
him a regular income which he might not ordinarily get.

A retail outlet, particularly a large one, knows how many
dollars each square foot of space should earn. If the store
has a weak department they will often consider getting rid
of it and putting in something suggested by a concessionaire.
If it's unique enough, such as baked goods, it might help
draw in many more customers for the business.

A concession can be exciting and rewarding. If you decide
that you want to investigate this business, the first thing you
must do is to decide what type of concession you want to
run. This may depend on the area you choose as to whether
or not the service you have in mind is workable, that is, in
demand. If there is no service, or products of the type you
visualize available in the town, then you are well on your
way.

Your next step is to locate an establishment in which you
can get space. Wholesalers will very often give excellent
credit terms to the person who is going to open a concession
in a well-known store. The distributors or manufacturers
want extra sales and they know the advantages of taking
space in a going concern.

Like all potential ideas, your preliminary check is extremely important. The more carefully this is done, the more
likely you are to succeed.

This Old Idea Can Be The "Key" to Profits

On the subject of concessions, key-making machines fit in
very well. If you can get a location in a busy shopping center,
for example, your profits could be very substantial. As in
other types of concessions, you could operate either on a
percentage basis or on a straight rental agreement.

It is not always necessary to be on duty at all times. The
owner of the concession might come in at specified times.
The manager of the retail outlet or other person could take
any orders and hold them for attention when the keymaker

comes in. This can certainly become a spare-time or second-income business. How well a person does will depend upon how heavy the passing traffic is.

43

Green Acres and Green Money

Morris J. had fifty acres of vacant land. He was paying taxes and it wasn't earning any real money. He had one small deal where a farmer came and cut the hay. The farmer kept half the crop in return for his labor and gave Morris a few dollars for the balance of the crop. But this hardly paid the taxes on the acreage.

One day Morris had an idea. He contacted a vegetable distributor and together they worked out a plan. The distributor would plow the fifty acres and plant tomatoes. The deal was that the wholesaler would have thirty-five acres and Morris would have fifteen.

Once the tomatoes started to ripen, Morris would run a classified ad offering them at a special price if people picked their own. He told me that a "take" of $200 a day at the height of the season was not unusual. Many people bought $15 worth of tomatoes for pickling and canning. All he had to do was to station himself at a little table near the entrance where the tomatoes were growing, and weigh them as the people came out of his field.

Planting, spraying, or other necessary field work was done over the entire property by the vegetable man.

"I think that proves," said Morris, "that you can make money out of almost anything if you go about it right."

Morris, who is in his late sixties, is now considering growing strawberries on another piece of vacant land and offering the same proposition to someone in the fruit business.

44

What Are They Doing Now?

Most medium and large-sized companies have a growing number of retirees on pension. Many firms put out, or have considered publishing, a periodical mentioning what these former employees are doing now.

A check I made showed that some of these publications are published quarterly, and others semi-annually. They usually run eight to twelve pages an issue. Some are tabloid size, others smaller. They have names such as *The Seniors' Star (Sun), Retirees Review, Retirees News,* etc.

Beside each news item carried, which runs to 100 words or more, is a photo of the retiree.

News covers such things as vacation trips, moving to new areas, new grandchildren, secondary jobs or businesses entered into, awards won, participation in sporting events, etc. These magazines are sent to the former employees without charge.

Normally, an outside person is chosen to put out the publication, rather than a company employee. Sometimes a public relations firm takes on the contract, but even then someone is often hired to do the work. Usually a senior citizen is chosen because of his or her sympathetic approach and understanding of senior citizens' interests. The work is usually done on a fee-per-issue basis. About $250 to $500 is a common figure for an average size of issue and travel costs are extra. The reporter also gets an extra payment for any photos taken. This is a pleasant type of work and is becoming more popular all the time.

In some cases the operator looks after the paste-up of material, printing, and mailing. The charge, of course, is then considerably higher than for just straight editing, and depends on time and outside costs.

You would be working with the personnel department which would supply names and addresses of retirees. Your job would be to contact them for information on their doings. Picnics, dances, holidays, and banquets for company retirees would be important events to be covered.

45

Unpainted Desks Are in Big Demand

If you want to find out if there is a demand for low-priced student desks, run a classified ad offering one for sale. A couple of hours after the paper comes out, you will probably find that you could have sold a dozen desks.

At department stores and chains, three-drawer pine desks run about $100, while plywood models are less. While they are called students' desks, they may be used for different jobs from laying out stamps to being a typing table.

If you are handy with a saw and hammer, you can turn out these students' desks very quickly and find a ready market for them. Three feet long by eighteen inches wide is a popular size with two drawers on the right side. The height would be twenty-nine inches.

An examination of a finished desk shows that it is put together quite quickly. Varnishing hides any defects in the wood and nailheads. Some stores sell desks finished in enamel which adds slightly to your cost, but also gives you the opportunity of selling a variety of colors to an outlet.

Your biggest cost is the wood. Some outlets, such as lumberyards dealing in wood, will cut it to your size. Wood costs can be reduced considerably if you are buying in quantity.

Some people who turn out desks in a garage or basement frequently add a line of shelves. However, demand for these latter items is not as big as for desks.

One important point is that if you are near your retail outlets, then it would be a saving on transportation. And don't overlook the many direct sales you could make to friends and neighbors, and through classified ads.

46

Mini-Sized Toys Are Fun to Make

There can be both enjoyment and profit in the home man-
ufacturing of such things as midget-sized furniture, doll houses,
garages, cars, animals, barns, and other items. I know two
chaps who have been doing this type of work, and they find
it relaxing, and at times quite profitable.

One retiree has built doll houses that are three stories in
height; the actual size is about two feet high. He builds them
in different designs, and also makes the furniture. He works
with wood, and he paints the items to resemble actual furniture. He makes pianos which are about four inches in length.
Sofas, stoves, tables, etc., all are on a similar-sized scale.
Both ends of a doll house can be left open so that children
can place the furniture to their liking.

Other popular sets are barns with wooden animals. Stalls
can be built in the barn, and front doors can be made to
swing open for children's arranging of the stock. Animals, as
other toys, can be largely block models, rather than exact
duplicates.

Garages and fire stations are very popular. Cars and trucks
would also be supplied as part of the set.

The prices of sets depends on time involved, size, and
other factors. Orders are gotten from friends and neighbours.
Stores will often display one or more sets. They would expect
a profit of about one-third. Prices such us $25 and even $50
are not unusual.

When painting articles, choose non-toxic paints. Avoid lead-
based paints. Check the paint manufacturer's information on
the container.

Convenience stores are often good outlets for specialty

items. As an example, a senior citizen I know produced a five-dollar children's book and it went well in these handy stores.

47

Farmhouse Holidays Are Growing in Popularity

*I*f you live in the city but have often wanted to buy a small farm, and you need an income from it to pay the mortgage, one way you could do it is as follows.

Sylvia W. bought a five-acre hobby farm with a fairly good house on it for $30,000. It was located five miles from a town and fifty from the nearest city.

About three years ago she began fixing up the old house which had four bedrooms. She papered, painted, and decorated the rooms and then began advertising summer vacations.

She was surprised at the response she got. In fact, for June, July, and August, she was completely filled. She offered three meals as well as accommodation for $15 daily per person, double occupancy. Sometimes, people would bring their children and they would have a great time wandering around. There was a golf course ten miles away which offered a further recreational attraction.

In addition Sylvia made a list of historical and other points of interest within a twenty-five-mile range and this helped her guests find something interesting to do. There were also nearby lakes and streams for fishing and swimming.

One retired couple doing this offers guests a choice of either having a lunch they can take with them on a day's outing, rather than returning at noon. An Ontario area, Bancroft, north of Belleville, offers tourists the opportunity of visiting old surface mines in search of various types of quartz.

Rates you charge will of course have to be based on current costs in your area. With the high costs of hotels and motels many people are interested in more simple, inexpensive vacations. Even if you live in a small town and have a couple of rooms available, you might try taking in "boarders" during the holiday season. And if your area offers winter sports, you may want to cash in on this season too.

48

There's Money in Store Demonstrations

A California man makes excellent money demonstrating and selling unusual items. He specializes in working with smaller department and variety stores.

When I met this man he was selling battery-operated shoe polishers at $4.95. He confided that they cost $2.50 in gross lots, and he gave the store a dollar on each one sold. They checked the stock arriving so there was no problem re sales totals. He said that on a good day he could move fifty to seventy-five units. He would spend Thursday, Friday, and Saturday at a location. On other days he ordered stock, and checked for other locations.

He has also worked church bazaars and various trade shows.

He said that "action" items that could be demonstrated with movement are the easiest to sell.

Many low-priced products which lend themselves to demonstration or novelty use come from the Orient. There are importers in the larger cities, and the Yellow Pages will give you the addresses of novelty wholesalers.

I purchased a frying pan, and a saucepan some ten years ago from a man demonstrating a line at a restaurant trade show in Toronto. The products were heavy duty and prices were higher than the light-weight items found in most stores commanded. This man did well because he knew how to demonstrate. You have to find the sales angle and promote it. This cookware would move slowly if only displayed in a store, so this sales person worked primarily in association shows.

I know another fellow who sold paintings in department stores. He would run a two-day sale, Friday and Saturday. At one such event I attended in Eaton's, Montreal, he had a very large area on the top floor of the building. Hundreds of paintings were displayed, many brought over from Europe for the event. The average price was around $100.

Articles sold in this manner are often bought by the salesperson on consignment as it is not known how such products will sell.

I once made a living selling Christmas greeting cards at church bazaars in October and November. I had little money and a manufacturer very kindly gave me all the stock I needed. I paid him once a week. The church or other social organization got 25 percent of sales.

Stores won't be interested in something similar or the same as any item they already sell. It really has to be something unique.

Introduce Interesting New Products

Many manufacturers and distributors employ men and women on a salary basis to introduce new products in their line. I met a woman in New Jersey who worked three days a week in retail liquor outlets. Her job was to invite customers to sample a new liquor being introduced by a distillery. Demonstrations or sampling are good ways to get people to try new products.

If a salesperson can tell the retailer that the company will hold a demonstration, stores are likely to place larger orders.

A letter to a distributor or manufacturer suggesting that you are interested in this work might prove worthwhile. Classified ads are sometimes run by companies looking for such help. House-to-house sales programs are sometimes held. I worked for a flour company who were introducing a new flour. The sales group carries metal baking pans. The person coming to the door was told that if she bought a seven-pound bag of this flour she would get a free baking dish. All she had to do was go to the store of her choice. She then gave us the name of her grocer and her address. She got a copy of the order and so did the group manager. This chap would have no difficulty getting enough orders to fill customer demands. We in turn received thirty-five cents an order. The lady got a copy of the order which she presented for her flour (at a special introductory price) and free pan.

It was a great little money-maker, while it lasted, for everyone concerned.

49

Rent Out Rooms for Special Events

There seems to be a continuous demand by various groups for space to hold special events. This might be club meetings, card parties, showers, private office parties, and other events.

To many small groups, of say ten to twenty people, the cost of renting a commercial hall is too steep, but a private home would be ideal.

You would need a large living room, or combination living room and dining area. Some groups meet weekly, while others meet monthly.

A dollar to $1.50 per head is an average charge. One hotel I visited, which has a room where a singles group of thirty meets twice a month, charges $3 per person, or a minimum of $50. A coffee urn is kept bubbling on a side table, along with powdered cream, sugar, paper cups, and cookies. A private home might find a charge of about $25 an evening very acceptable.

50

Antique Dealers Need Representatives

Antique retailers and auction houses have to have merchandise if they are to stay in business. If the subject interests you, try teaming up with a dealer.

You will get advice as to what kind of antiques to buy, areas to look for them, the price range, and what your percentage will be. You will probably have to study the antiques on display at retail stores and auction rooms to get an idea as to what it is all about. The work is interesting and can be profitable.

One couple in the Maritimes who is working with an auction house got a call for buggies and other types of carriages used in the early years of the 20th century. They began calling on farmers and were surprised that carriages of all types were hidden away in barns. There were sleighs, too, which they were able to buy. They picked up these articles for $50 to $100.

Profit depends on various factors—condition, age, type, and how far it had to be transported. On the auction block, an article that the couple paid $100 for might bring anywhere from $500 to $1,000 once it has been repaired and polished. This type of buggy or carriage is often used outside a motel to attract attention, and people with large lawns will often buy one to add an air of graciousness to their premises.

Libraries frequently have books specializing in the type of antiques for which you will be looking. If you are not already aware of it, different dealers specialize in different types (and ages) of antiques. As far as payment is concerned, some may put you on a monthly drawing account to cover expenses or otherwise help you defray your expenses while searching for merchandise.

51

Start a Senior Citizens' Orchestra

*I*f, over the years, you have played a musical instrument, you might consider forming a combo group. There are disc jokkeys with records and tape collections who play at parties, dances, and weddings but many people would prefer live entertainment if available. You wouldn't necessarily have to play the latest rock and roll music, but rather you could specialize in the old standards which are always in demand.

This would certainly keep you busy with practising and playing two or three nights a week. Afternoon concerts could also be organized. A drummer I know plays at a club. He retired from his regular office job some time ago and thoroughly enjoys his new vocation.

Another chap, Charles Lawrence, until recently played saxophone a few times a month around the Durham, Owen Sound, Ontario area, and he is a very young seventy-nine.

So, even if you're a little rusty on the trumpet, drums, or piano, you'll come back fast. A classified ad in the local paper advertising your "group" might work wonders!

Classified ads could also be used to get any additional musicians you need for your group.

52

You Can Learn to Tune Pianos

A man in his sixties began earning a good second income as a result of visits to the library. He began learning the art of how-to-tune pianos. His first introduction to the subject was from a book.

If you have ever wanted to have a piano tuned you probably know how difficult it is to find someone to do it. Moreover, the charge is quite high. This person had an old piano at home which he used for practical study and, in addition to this, some library books helped him to become proficient enough to tackle a few jobs. Soon word-of-mouth advertising got him all the business he could handle.

Today there is a demand for almost every type of product and every type of service. One lady of sixty-nine learned how to knit shawls and ponchos. She creates exotic designs and just can't keep up with the demand. She gets as much as $100 for one of her creations, and has developed her skill to such a degree that she can turn out a poncho in a couple of days.

53

Writing Letters—Pleasant, Profitable

Writing letters is a simple matter for most people. Yet there is a steady demand for this service from people and some businesses.

One woman, who lives near the Quebec border, not far from New York State, says she writes letters for people (and stores) and gets $2.60 a letter. The letters she writes for stores are at Christmastime. Children write to the store's Santa Claus, and this lady reads and answers the letters which stores send her. She gets most of her business by advertising under "personals."

Most people will "rough out" a letter and mail it along with a check to the letter writer. The finished letter and a photocopy are mailed to the sender. These are usually business letters, personal and family letters, etc.

Some people prefer to have their letters typed and this can be mentioned in the ad. An ad like this tells everything: "Letters written professionally. Typed or handwritten. Price, address."

Letters running over a page should be charged a higher rate.

Forwarding Mail Service

If you let it be known through classified ads that you will forward mail, you could develop this as an additional service. Customers usually send sealed, addressed letters along with payment to the mailer. Forwarding mail to foreign countries should involve an extra charge.

Let's say someone in Toronto wants some letters mailed from Los Angeles, and you live in Los Angeles or can provide service from there, then you could offer this service. Your advertisement would read: "Your letters mailed from Los Angeles, $1 per letter. Address." In quantity, the price would drop.

54

Money Does Grow on Trees

I once met a man from Tasmania, an island state of Australia. He told me that he makes money by creating "apple figures." The apple is cut away, leaving only the center core section. This is then placed in the sun to dry out. Once the core has hardened, this entrepreneur takes a sharp knife and cuts out little heads. Then the core is sprayed or painted with varnish.

My acquaintance from Tasmania said that the results are quite interesting. All sorts of wizened little figures and faces take shape. He makes a flat wooden base on which the apple figure is mounted. Then he usually adds wooden ornaments such as animals, trees, a building, and other objects to create an entire scene.

He says his art sells well in boutiques at $25-$50, depending on how much time is spent in the creation of the piece. A store will take one-third of the total amount.

55

He Grows "Penguins" as a Money-Making Hobby

*I*n eastern countries, where refrigerators are scarce, gourds are used to keep water cool. Here in Canada, the shmoo-like variety of melon serves a more decorative purpose, and provides a hobby for many amateur craftsmen.

Philip Kieran, a retired artist of Beaurepaire, Quebec, began to "look into" gourds some ten years ago after a friend had given him a handful of seeds.

"I was so impressed with the funny shapes that the gourds took," says Kieran, "that I soon became a rabid gourd fan. Since then, I have done a great deal of experimenting, in both the growing and the finishing."

Planted in the spring, gourds ripen just before the first frost. Then they are dried for several months in a light, warm, well-ventilated storage space. There are hard-shelled and soft-shelled gourds—Kieran says the hard-shelled variety is best for the types of object he makes. These include lamps and wall-masks of birds and animals.

Once the gourd is thoroughly dry, the inside seeds and pulp can easily be removed with a knife. Cutting the head or bottom off the gourd, depending on what you are making, is done with a hacksaw. Gourds in their raw state are rough both outside and inside.

Various grades of sandpaper and steel wool will smooth these surfaces down. Kieran's other tools and materials include household cement, enamels, plastic wood, brushes, fretsaws, wood files, a drill, a hammer and a hook-pointed linoleum knife.

Encouraging the "Penguins"
Gourds are so lifelike that each seems to signal its own

category. On occasion Kieran channels this talent by growing a seed inside a bottle, and then gently breaking the bottle when the seed reaches maturity. This produces "penguins" or other desired shapes.

In the early stages it is possible to tie the gourds or place a tape around them. This also results in some fascinating shapes. The stem is an important part—it forms the beak in bird models—and to make sure that the stem will remain in good condition some growers use trellises to hold the growing gourds.

Kieran sells his gourd figures to gift and souvenir shops, particularly those catering to tourists. The demand is so heavy for some kinds, such as penguins, that Kieran can't keep up with it.

"I often make a rough sketch on a piece of paper," he says, "before starting to paint a gourd. Brilliant enamels allow plenty of room for imagination, and even an amateur can come up with some striking designs."

Contrasting Colors

Kieran's wife Elizabeth, who does much of the painting, says she prefers solid colors. For example: take one fat gourd, cut the top off. Paint that black and the bottom a brilliant red, and you have a bon-bon dish which really is unusual. A contrasting color can be used to paint the inside of the gourds.

Says Mrs. Kieran: "Gourds are easy to grow, requiring practically no effort; yet with a little attention and imagination they can be turned into lovely gifts. I can think of no hobby, especially for the winter, which gives so much pleasure and profit for so little outlay."

If you don't want to bother growing gourds, they can be purchased from a seed house. It is wise to make sure that the gourds used are free of cracks and unsightly knots. Remember, you can't change the basic shape of a gourd, so you must plan the part this particular one will play. Frequently, though, a nose for a face can be added by the judicious use of plastic wood.

But why not try growing gourds in your garden? You might get "penguins."

If you have a garden, gourd seeds can be purchased at almost all seed retailers. The cost averages forty-nine cents for a package of thirty-six seeds. Most packages contain a variety of seeds that will grow into different shapes, and sizes.

In the fall many food stores carry the mature gourd and they sell for approximately $1.49 for a dozen. Some commercial gardeners also sell gourds and here your choice is likely to be larger.

56

The Stained Glass Business

Over the past few years, there has been quite a swing toward stained glass of all kinds: Tiffany lamps and windows, and ornaments such as flowers and birds.

This hobby could be of interest to retirees because the work can be done at home. Courses in stained glass are available from firms which sell supplies, and individuals who themselves have become experts. Stained glass instruction is popular at many colleges and high schools. This is a noncredit course and in many areas both evening and afternoon classes are available. Rates range from $25 to $150 or more per course.

One instructor told me that his usual charge is $5 per student for a one-hour lesson. This instructor further stated that out of every ten people taking the course, two become proficient enough to make money at it. Three will continue with the work for its hobby interest, while five will take the course to meet new people and see what it's all about. This teacher said that on the average there was one commercial shop selling supplies and teaching the craft for about every 125,000 people in larger cities. Montreal, for example, has about fifteen combination instruction and retail outlets.

Lamps may retail from around $75 to $800, depending on their size and style. Gift pieces are priced from $15 up, while windows bring varying prices. Small wall and window hangers (made from scrap glass) are very popular as gifts.

The cost for a set of tools and a grinder runs about $250. Breakage of glass is high. You should figure your costs for big jobs (for material) at about 20 percent of your selling price. However, on small pieces like novelty items, you can use scrap glass, and an item say ten by twelve inches sells for $15, might take $1 worth of materials. Some people report incomes of up to $200 from just a few hours work.

There are books in most libraries and book stores on how to create stained glass articles. A corner of a basement is a good place to work. The process is not noisy or dirty.

57

Night Man Wanted!

Young people don't usually care to work at night—they say it interferes with their love life! Most of the seniors I know seem to have just about as much love life as the kids, but they don't talk about it as much.

Anyway, if you like night work, there are often night jobs available which are ideal for senior citizens. One popular vocation is night desk clerk at a small hotel or motel.

In addition to contacting hotels, you might also write to various large- and medium-sized businesses telling them of your willingness to work at night. The results could be worthwhile. There are also certain types of work which, because of lack of space, less noise, etc., are more easily and efficiently performed at night.

If you only wanted to work two or three nights a week, you might consider job-sharing. This is gaining in popularity and often works in well with the needs of retirees.

Sometimes advertising appears in the newspapers in the classified section under "help wanted." If you want to work out of town, you could contact the hotel association serving your area.

58

Prints from Hong Kong

*R*eg M. of Vancouver, B.C., is retired and has built a profitable spare-time business selling Hong Kong prints (scenes) by mail. The prints are unframed and shipped by him to his customers in cardboard tubes. The scenes are full color and pertain to the Orient. They sell for between $6 and $15 depending on the size. The wholesale price is about 25 percent of the retail price, says Reg.

The main value of such a business is that the product is light to mail, there is almost no possibility of damage, stock on hand does not become outdated, and it is possible to build a good repeat business. And repeat business means additional profits with few if any additional selling costs, i.e., advertising.

Finding your wholesale source is the biggest job. You may start by purchasing from wholesale sources in major cities. These would be firms which deal in import items. A letter to the Hong Kong or Singapore Chambers of Commerce will also bring some information. You could visit art galleries where prints are sometimes displayed, or check with retailers who handle such lines.

How to Advertise, How to Sell

Reg says he gets most of his business by advertising in American magazines devoted to home decoration, and his ads run from two-inch columns to a sixth of a page. You might also try to use the classified sections of such magazines.

Prints are bought primarily by younger people who want to introduce a novelty effect to their homes or apartments. To gain interest you may have to offer a free folder which would contain pictures of the prints you are offering. Reg says he runs at least one picture (three inches by five inches) in full color in his folder to give prospects an idea of what the finished work looks like. You might offer a choice of a dozen with one free if two or more prints are ordered at one time. Customers very often reorder either for themselves or for gifts.

A second sales opportunity would be to offer prints to local retailers. If a print which retails at $6 costs you $1.50, you could offer it to a retailer for $3 and both of you would be making a good profit. You would be selling in lots of from six to twelve prints and you would have no postage to pay.

59

Teaching Bridge Offers Many Benefits

Over the past few years bridge has become extremely popular with senior citizens, so if you have a good knowledge of the game, you might consider becoming a teacher.

I discussed how bridge is taught with one lady who is close to eighty and has been teaching bridge ever since she lost her husband some twenty years ago. Here is what she told me: "I charge $3 a lesson. It used to be $2. The lessons run from 8 to 10 P.M. I have two tables going and that means eight people. I usually have enough students for two tables four or five nights a week. Many of the people are retirees, and this is what I specialize in. Many regard it as a social event, and return month after month. I teach various types of bridge. One lady has been attending my classes regularly for ten years. I always serve coffee and cookies. My main function is to go from table to table giving pointers and explain how a poor play has been made.

"Teaching bridge has helped me psychologically too. And as far as income is concerned, this has helped me pay off my home, and also build a fascinating circle of friends. I seem to get all the students I can handle just by word-of-mouth advertising."

So here is a fascinating money-making idea that would probably be very much appreciated in your area. Bridge lessons could be given during afternoons if this is more convenient.

60

Tying Fishing Flies Makes Money

*F*ishing flies have to be tied, and as far as I can determine, the work is done just about the same today as it was a hundred years ago. You use a small vise, a pair of small sharp scissors, feathers of various kinds, tying thread, and various sizes of hooks.

You will have to get a book showing the most popular flies or check out local sporting goods stores. They will give you an idea of wholesale and retail prices, popular patterns, and possibly sources of material. You can also check the yellow pages for suppliers who can sell you materials in bulk.

You don't have to have small, delicate hands to tie flies. One retired gentleman weighs well over 200 pounds and has hands the size of the proverbial hams. Yet he ties flies with great speed and agility, and as a result earns a tidy second income.

Some salmon and trout fishermen spend long, cold winters making their own flies, but most fishermen prefer to buy them. A fly which can be tied in ten minutes by an expert will often retail for $2.50.

Flies sell better when displayed. The easiest way is to attach flies to a card about two inches square. You may have identification rubber stamps made if you're only offering a few patterns. A thread can be used to attach them to the cards.

I met a Japanese man at a trade show who made spinners and sold them at six for $5. These were encased in small cellophane envelopes. Flies can also be handled this way.

If you get a reputation for making flies that catch fish people will be contacting you constantly. But chances are,

at least at the beginning, that you'll have to let fishermen
know what you have.

The first thing to do is contact tackle shops. If you can
rubber stamp your cards "Made in Canada," this will help
sales. I have found that imported tackle, particularly nylon
or gut, is not always strong enough for our heavy, powerful
fish. Cold waters build fighters!

Retailers will want 40 percent. They'll prefer to take your
stock on consignment.

If you can display and possibly speak at angling meetings
you'll become known. Calls at fishing camps could be helpful.
And, of course, if you attend outdoor shows this can help.
These shows are held in principal Canadian cities, in the
spring. Read the three or four Canadian outdoor magazines
found on the newsstands, and contact the angling and hunting associations in your area. Your local sporting goods store
should have the names and addresses of association executives.

If you can work the sportsmen's shows, or have existing
booths sell your line, you could move a lot of goods.

Advertising won't help you unless you have a reputation
or can use large spaces and get national distribution. Your
name is just another name in hundreds of tackle items, so
fishermen aren't impressed by a few words of copy. But if
the prospect can see and touch the item, plus get a little
sales pitch, that's different.

Handmade fishing rods are in demand too. A chap in our
town buys his trout and salmon rods from a small maker in
Scotland. The price? About $250 each.

With all the machine-made equipment pouring out, there
is always a demand for the handmade personal item.

61

Don't Let Your Talents and Knowledge Go To Waste!

Music and scholastic subjects which can be taught in either your home, or a student's, are usually worth considering by seniors. If you play a musical instrument, particularly an organ or a piano, you could probably find students of all ages who would be interested in getting some training. And, of course, if you can visit the student's home you will be even more popular, as this is a service hard to come by. One person charges $8 for a half-hour of organ lessons.

Even people with just a fair knowledge of music are offering lessons. Retirees like to engage a teacher to help them brush up on their technique. Some teachers are able to help students by teaching them to play chords and melody by ear, thus eliminating the need to learn scales which older students often find distasteful.

General subjects such as art, advertising, writing, and dozens of other topics can make a good income for teachers who will offer their services. If you are knowledgeable in a subject, why let it go to waste just because you have retired from the business.

About five years ago I offered six evening lessons in writing. I ran a small ad once, sent circulars to a group of writers, and arranged a meeting place. On the first night, thirty-five people showed up and thirty signed for the course. Part of the training consisted of taking any interested students with me on an actual interview for an article assignment.

The lessons, twice a month, $10 a lesson, became almost a social event, with stops after for coffee and hot dogs. Students (ages from twenty to retirement) would tell of work they had done, or read something they had written, which helped other students and, of course, the teacher.

The Artistic Touch

One woman in the Midwest had a hobby of painting landscapes. While she worked she gave her paintings to friends and relatives, but when she retired from the bank, she decided that maybe she could do something a little more practical with her art. She knew she could improve herself, so she took a course. Her technique improved and she became much happier with her work.

She spent a lot of time visiting different places to get subject material such as ships in canals, old farmhouses, and rustic bridges. She would often paint the same scene from different angles. If she saw a scene she didn't have time to sketch, or if it was getting close to sundown, she would take a Polaroid photograph of the subject and do the actual painting whenever she was in the mood. This sort of thing was great for her art when the weather was poor.

When she felt her canvases had reached the right professional plateau, she called on art buyers at department stores, galleries, and a few boutiques. Her work was soon hanging in a number of places and while sales weren't a daily affair, at least they were encouraging. One art dealer suggested she spend $25 to have a resume typed up. She did this, and attached this little "biog" to each canvas. Sales went up remarkably. One dealer complimented her: "Most artists, in all fields," he said, "are too modest about their work."

62

Making and Selling Candles Has Possibilities

There is a continuous demand for candles of all types, and many people collect them as a hobby. Waxes and molds are available as well as instructions on making candles at home. Gift shops are constant buyers of candles and you might find it reasonably easy to get customers.

Candles normally sell from $5 up. Retailers require a discount of 33 to 40 percent. Libraries have books on how to make candles and these often include a list of sources of supply. Candle manufacturers often have a department which sells molds, wax, and other materials.

It is the craft-person's originality which will in large measure determine how successful the venture will be. One couple working together produced some striking candles. The steps for making one model are relatively simple and are outlined below:

You take a clean, empty milk carton and fill it with cracked ice. In the center insert a regular, long, white wax candle with only its wick protruding above the top of the box or carton. The final step is to pour hot wax over the chips or blocks of ice. The wax may be colored or plain. Before the ice has had a chance to melt, the wax will have reached the bottom of the carton and formed a base. You will of course pour in sufficient wax to reach the top of the container. Put the unit in the refrigerator or other cool place to harden. When you remove the cardboard your block of wax contains holes of all shapes and sizes which are now filled with water from the melted ice. If you use your imagination you will come up with many original mold ideas that can make you a star in the candle business.

63

You Can Make Money with Old Eye Glasses

*I*t seems that these days there is a use for just about everything, no matter how old it might be.

A girl who is confined to her home developed this idea. She contacts opticians and eye specialists and asks them if they would give her their old eye glasses or lenses. Her only interest is the lens.

She makes beautiful pendants. She paints pictures of all kinds on the lens, while on some others she does straight designs. Very often the lens has a pinhole in it so that it can be attached to a chain which she supplies. If the lens has no hole, a jeweler will drill them for her.

Friends, neighbors, relatives, and gift shops buy just about all the pendants she can turn out. She gets the chains complete with clasps and has them available in different designs. These can usually be purchased in quantity from wholesale jewelers.

It is a type of work which is interesting and financially rewarding. Moreover, there is little money required to get started. Retail prices run from $10 to $50 and up, depending on the amount of work, and cost of the chain. The wholesale price is normally double or triple the investment.

64

Ten Services That Are Needed by Retailers

A retailer has to wear many hats even if he has an assistant or two, and this can result in a steady flow of interesting work for retirees.

The first and most obvious need is for part-time sales help, but apart from this just look at the different types of work which have to be done regularly in a busy store, and see where you might fit in. All of the following positions are part-time.

There's window dressing. Men and women with a flair for artistic backgrounds should do well at this. Windows should be changed every two weeks at least.

Interior displays that will move merchandise are always needed if a merchant is going to keep sales high.

Collections are an important part of all retail businesses. This can be done by invoice and telephone. Payment to you can be made on an hourly basis, or by a percentage of monies collected. Older accounts bring larger commissions. Year-old accounts often earn 50 percent of the amount collected. The older the account the higher the commission or the percentage paid to the collector. Normal percentages (three months to six months overdue), run 10 to 25 percent.

If you have a background in advertising media, you may be able to help retailers in your area. Most retailers are heavily dependent on local radio and print independent advertising.

Publicity means getting your client's name in the paper and on the air without charge to "the boss." There are many ways to get free publicity: perhaps the store is having an anniversary sale, or a contest is being held, or possibly some other event worthy of publicity is "born" in the mind of the public relations boss. One publicity person found a stock of old razors, and other hardware in a warehouse. The goods had been stored for seventy-five years. They were brought out, put on display, and publicity notices were sent out. The press picked up this news and the result was that the store disposed of all of the souvenir merchandise it had. People purchased the items as curios.

If your client does some advertising, then the publicity is easier to achieve.

Showcard writing is often necessary and if you can turn your hand to this, you will find plenty of business.

Telephone solicitation of business can be a profitable operation if you work with local merchants in a small town. Let's say everyone knows the local hardware store and it receives a large shipment of refrigerators. You are authorized to offer them by phone at a certain percentage off the list price. In fact, the special could also be announced in the local newspaper. Very often a special like this can be arranged by a smart merchandising person who finds out about manufacturers' overstocks and then approaches a store. There need be no cash outlay. The store can usually get a sample model for thirty days, and then you begin to promote it. The regular price could be $400, and on the basis of a good order, possibly stretched over three months, the merchant might pay $200 a unit. So you split the profit with you paying for any advertising. There are endless deals that can be worked out if you start thinking along these lines.

Delivery service is an essential part of many retail operations. However, because of the added work of hiring a staff member and providing a vehicle (taxes, deductions, paperwork), many merchants would much rather "farm" the work out. You are your own boss, provide your own delivery unit, and pay all costs. You can often arrange to work only certain hours a day, such as mornings or afternoons. Payment would have to be worked out as to a delivery or hourly basis.

One lady delivers in the afternoons for a pharmacy. She has a small car and pays necessary costs herself.

Maintenance Service
This is not something that you might want to do yourself,

but you could engage others, particularly reliable, well-recommended, serious high school students.

Have you ever noticed how some stores have a bright, shiny appearance, while others seem to be musty?

The latter are probably "broomed" over lightly at the start of the day, while the others receive a professional going-over, with twice-a-week floor washing.

You could get a half dozen or more merchants to use your service. It could also include windows which are always a problem.

Some big cleaning businesses, including maintenance of highrise office buildings, have been started by entrepreneurs who started with a few local businesses.

The best thing that you can do is decide which areas you wish to specialize in. Usually a couple of departments is adequate; these could be advertising and publicity. Once you've chosen your field, spend some time reading up on it. Remember that merchants in smaller cities and towns are better prospects than those in large areas. Besides, your competition will probably be nil in the smaller areas.

You could choose a number of different types of stores to work with. Grocery stores (keep away from the chains) have their own setups, but drug stores, bookstores, hardware dealers, sporting goods retailers, and other outlets are usually good prospects.

In six months you'll not only be an expert in the subjects you have chosen, but also very knowledgeable in the businesses you are working with.

In addition to retailers, you might wish to also consider wholesalers and manufacturers. It's all a big field, and the beauty of it for retirees is that you can devote as little or as much time as you wish to it.

65

Start Your Own Local Newspaper

One of the most interesting, and reasonably profitable businesses I ever engaged in, was the publishing of a quarterly suburban newspaper. It is the type of business that almost any senior can get started in, and the cash outlay need not be more than three or four hundred dollars. Of course you don't have to bring out just a quarterly, you can go monthly, or even weekly.

There is hardly an area which doesn't need another paper, even if there already are one or more. The world has become so big and crowded that much local news has no place to be heard.

In the old days, the dailies carried local, personal items, often with photographs. Then, as they became part of chains, they carried more syndicate news because it was cheaper and easier to get.

Then the weeklies took up the slack, and they began carrying the local news that was formerly the province of the dailies. But as communities expanded, so did the weekly paper, and once again many of the little local news items were dispensed with by the growing weeklies, many of which too became part of larger publishing chains.

All this, of course, had considerably affected many small advertisers. When an advertiser used a daily he was often paying for coverage twenty and thirty or more miles away, but people wouldn't travel that far. The only merchants who benefited were those who had chains of stores. They were quick to place ads in areas where dailies had heavy circulation, hence their cost for advertising for each store was extremely low. If the daily charged $2,000 per page and a company had twenty stores, all the retailer was paying was

$100 per page per store. But the little merchant with one store was paying a very high rate for his ad. Some dailies offered split runs, and part circulation at reduced rates, but it was still expensive.

So the local merchants found the answer in the local weekly, but today many weeklies in suburban areas have upped circulation and ad rates to a point where the small store owner has been casting around for other means of advertising. Mailing out circulars had become popular, but then increasing postal rates have made this method less popular.

So here is an opportunity for retirees—a little tabloid. When I stopped publishing mine the cries from advertisers and readers could be heard over the three square miles of territory it covered.

Five Steps to Get Started in Publishing a Small Tabloid
The first thing you are going to say is, "But I don't know anything about the business." This should make you very happy—just think of the fun you're going to have learning. And age doesn't matter. I knew a woman, Margaret Bartlett, of Boulder, Colorado who ran a publication when she was in her late seventies.

I will give you five simple steps to follow, and if you do so I will guarantee you success.

First you choose a name. There are about fifty standard names for newspapers. Any name will do so long as it's not the same as the paper in your town or nearby area. If there is no *Gazette, Times, Post, Advocate, Examiner, Monitor, Express, News, Guardian, Herald*, etc., choose one of these. Just add your town's or district's name. If you live in Beantown, then call it the *Beantown Bulletin*, or *Banner.*

Secondly, don't be too classy. You haven't any competition, at least editorially. Keep your ad rates at about 25 to 35 percent of your printing cost. Next decide on the page size of your paper. It can be an eight-sheet tabloid, or a dozen sheets letterhead size. You can go to a copy center and have the paper reproduced on letterhead-sized sheets back-to-back, or you can go legal size (eight and one-half by fourteen inches) and fold.

A little local paper can be published for any area, so don't worry if you live in a large city. Say you live on 10th Avenue, and there is a nearby business section. Cover this area. It might be four blocks by six blocks. My little paper was in a city of 18,000 people. I covered about 2,000 homes—those closest to the merchants. There was already a weekly with 20,000 circulation ($1,000 a page for an ad) plus, of course, the big daily.

So let's say you decide on 2,000 circulation; go to printers and get prices. Shop around. Set your own type by typewriter. Paste in the copy and the ads. You can use a regular typewriter at the beginning, or rent a typesetting unit from IBM. You can sometimes buy used ones for five hundred dollars. If you can type you will have no trouble. If your wife is still talking to you up to this point, you can probably enlist her services. If you explain to the printer that you will supply camera-ready material, and all he has to do is print the thing, you should get a low price. Maybe you can sell him an ad and that will help.

Get him to paste up the name of your paper at the top of a tabloid sheet, and photocopy a few copies. He might charge you $5 but he shouldn't. You might become his best customer. Don't accept the first price you get. Try the big and the small printers. Your success will depend on the price you get.

You must work out your ad rates. If, for example, your printer is going to charge you $200 for four tabloid sheets, then you would charge about $200 a page. You are not going to sell all four pages—you'll need about half for editorial. When you have the dummy pasted up, draw out in pencil a collection of different size ads and write in the price. This way the prospective advertiser can see what size of ad he will get with the amount of money he wants to spend. Your page rate will probably be $200, while half a page will be $125 and other smaller sizes will be in proportion. There is a 5 to 10 percent discount for advertisers who come in regularly.

The Survey Is Important

Talk to the merchants, some of whom you will know, and conduct a survey. Get their reaction. You are giving them a prime audience. People right around the store. No waste circulation. Sure he's getting twenty times the circulation in the other paper for maybe a thousand dollars, but maybe half of it is waste. And because you are specializing in local news and photographs, your readership will be higher. On the first issue you should at least break even, and maybe make a profit. If there are shopping centers outside your circulation area, call on them too. They already draw from this market, so they may be interested in more advertising even if they are in a daily.

If you have a good credit rating your printer will probably let you pay him after your issue comes out and you have collected. You would be wise, before you start selling advertising, to have a sales sheet typed and printed by a copy center. The cost will be about $15 for 300. Print your display and classified rates, and mention your circulation area and local editorial approach.

Your bank will take a small ad. Head office tells managers to encourage local business. Other local merchants may be interested in placing ads too. Don't add circulation too quickly or you will be in the same position as the big daily and weekly.

I found a monthly was a good bet for a senior. You don't have to work too hard, yet you could cover local council and social events. Stick to local news. Give the paper away free at the beginning. Have school youngsters deliver it, or do it yourself.

You'll find the whole business exciting and, if handled right, the paper could be very profitable. You'll be surprised at all the knowledge and benefits that will accrue.

You will probably be editor and publisher. Appoint two or three retirees to get local news. They'll be delighted to do it for a subscription and the occasional conference-dinner.

66

Making Curtains and Drapes

*I*f you can sew, here is a real opportunity for you. A woman living on the west coast makes curtains and drapes to order and says she gets plenty of work, and is well paid for it. In fact, she says that she has three other women to whom she subcontracts work when she gets too busy.

There are millions of homes in the country, and most of them need curtains and drapes from time to time, and they have to be made by someone. There are some standard sizes available but most people prefer to buy the material and have the work made up for them.

The lady mentioned here started off by going to a store which sells curtains and drapery materials. She reports that these stores are frequently on the lookout for good seamstresses. She started doing the work by hand, but soon purchased a suitable sewing machine.

The stores will usually deliver the material to your home, along with sizes and any other specifications. Once you have made contact with a store, there can be a constant flow of work.

Obviously you have to be fast and good if you are going to make any real money at the business. If you have a knack for general needlework, most store people will fill you in on exactly what they want. It is to their advantage to have people like you working for them because they add at least 25 percent of your rate to what they charge. Classified ads will often bring you business.

You Might Consider a Drapery Store

One man operates a small shop where he takes order for making draperies. The only stock he carries are sample books.

If you wish, he will go to your home and take the measurements while you choose the color and pattern you want. Then he figures out the cost and collects a deposit which is usually half of the total amount. His next step is to go to the wholesale drapery firm and order the goods. He picks up the material, and then delivers it to one of the various women who do the work for him. He makes a profit on both the material and the labor.

It isn't necessary to take a whole store. You can rent a small space in a larger store, such as a dry cleaning establishment. You could even operate right from home. People telephone you and you visit them and show your samples.

Once again, this is a good business for retired men and women because you can set your own pace. You could also take on new interests, too, such as the making of slip covers for furniture. This involves showing sample materials and taking measurements. For any of this work, have the customer sign a contract which explains exactly what is being offered at what price. It's wise to attach a piece of the material to your contracts—the customer's and yours. Even factories can make mistakes in delivery numbers and there is no worse problem than when you proudly deliver a job and are looking forward to the check, and the lady says, "But I ordered the green and this is pink."

On any work of this nature you should get at least one-third payment in advance, and hopefully half.

There are retired piece workers who will make slip covers from home. A classified ad will usually reach them. Remember, almost any trade is filled with people of all ages who can do things but don't have the managerial expertise to go out and get the business. There are countless businesses being run by people who could never perform the service they are selling.

67

Want Your Windows Washed?

*I*t is surprising how much business is done by telephone solicitation. In the past six weeks I had my windows washed for $75 because a lady called me and suggested it. She would make 20 percent for five minutes work, or about $15. She had a man who worked for the firm she represented come to my house and give me the price. He got $10 and my signed contract. That afternoon two men came and did a good job in two hours. They got $30 total and picked up the check. They had their own truck, ladders, and pails. The owner of the business got the check which gave him $15.

I found out that he has six window-washing crews on the road. Each crew can do at least four jobs a day. That's a total of twenty-four window-washing jobs at $15 profit each for the boss. Got an adding machine?

He has no expenses except bookkeeping. The three women on the phones work from home, for themselves. The window washers and the estimators also work for themselves. They phone customers and tell them when they will arrive.

But that's not all. If you don't want your windows washed, maybe you'd like some painting or wallpapering work done. Or carpets washed? It's all operated on the same principle by the same boss. Only the crews change. I heard he started six years ago with the idea and last year did over $6 million!

There are people operating various telephone businesses and doing well. It's the type of opportunity that can be started prior to retirement and "is ready to go full blast" when you are.

Various services can be added. They include landscaping, cement work, chimney cleaning, painting, repairing mortar between bricks, roofing, tile laying, carpentry, rug installation, and looking after the garden, weeding, etc., when the owners go on holiday, plus other services which will come to mind.

People who want to work by telephone, and not go into the business as mentioned here, can contact any one of dozens of firms and get positions working from home. Personally, I have bought light bulbs, dry cleaning, a vacuum cleaner and various other products and services by telephone. I find it easier than going to a shopping center, standing around waiting to be served, and of course getting there and back, plus the cost.

The odd person you phone will snarl at you but so does your spouse on occasion.

68

Dinner for Twelve Coming Up!

How many times have you heard this, or a similar, remark? Mrs. Margaret A., has heard this remark hundreds of times, and she loves it because it puts money in her pocket. You see, Margaret, who is a senior, is also a good cook, and she caters to special parties.

She brought up a family of five in the town of 10,000 people where she lives. She knows many of the residents and she certainly knows cooking. "Not fancy cooking," she'll tell you, "just plain good-tasting cooking."

She doesn't handle ritzy affairs, or big parties. Her specialty is making dinner for a dozen or so guests, and she does all the work in the hostess's kitchen. Birthday parties, Christmas, New Year's, and Thanksgiving Day dinners are what she prides herself on.

She gets business by word-of-mouth advertising, and by placing a card on the announcement board in the local food market. If things get really slow she puts a classified ad in the local weekly. It usually reads, "Got guests coming for dinner? I'll cook the meal. Let's discuss it. Phone —."

A phone call leads to a meeting. Once it's established what the main course will be—turkey, chicken, beef, etc.—the rest falls into place. Margaret finds out how many guests there will be and then orders the food. The market she deals with delivers and charges $2 for this service. The hostess pays for the food when it arrives.

Margaret arrives in plenty of time to get the meal started so that it will be ready at the required time. She often brings her twenty-year-old granddaughter along to help with the serving and washup after. Margaret always leaves the kitchen

166

spotless, which is one reason she says she gets plenty of repeat business.

The rate she charges runs $5 to $7 an hour, sometimes a little more if there are extra guests. There is also an additional charge of about three hours for her assistant.

During July and August Margaret doesn't take on any "banquet assignments" but she is busy during most other periods. She will take as many as two jobs a week, but not more.

This type of service isn't restricted to women. There are also cases of men doing party cooking. They are a little more flambuoyant than Margaret, and wear the chef's white hat.

69

Consider Baking Christmas Cakes

A woman in a small town made the family Christmas cakes for years, and occasionally baked them for friends. She enjoyed the work and usually started the task about mid-November.

Then one year she decided to go into the business in a larger way. She figured raw ingredients at around $1 a pound, and so set the retail price for a cake at around $3. If a customer bought three cakes (three pounds), the price would be $8.

It was midsummer and she still had a couple of cakes left in the freezer, so she took them out, wrapped them individually, and began making a few calls. First she called on the bank manager. He admitted he had about 100 customers he usually liked to remember at Christmas. The lady had a little knife tucked in her purse along with some napkins, and had soon given her prospect a sliver of cake. He admitted it was very good. She agreed to wrap the cakes, and tie them with a red ribbon. When she left she had a confirming letter for 125 cakes at $3 each.

Next she called at the real estate office and they agreed to take twenty-five cakes. All day long she made calls. Some folks kidded her about Christmas in July, but by the time she had given away a whole cake she had orders for over 500. She had come out with an order pad, so everything was very businesslike.

She began buying ingredients in the summer because she figured they would be cheaper than at Christmastime.

A couple of weeks later she made a few more calls, this time on garages, a trust company, and an office supply firm. The lady discovered two important things. One was that most firms who have regular customers often like to remember them at Christmas. The second thing was that Christmas cakes are appreciated by just about everyone. Of course she began making them well ahead of Christmas. She figured how many a day she could make in her kitchen, and then multiplied it by the days needed to produce what she needed. One granddaughter helped whenever she could.

The cakes were carefully wrapped in aluminum foil. The cakes were then put in the freezer till required, when they were taken out, tied with ribbon, and delivered.

One year her son took some colored photographs of the cakes, and these were mailed to banks in nearby communities. A typed sheet, photocopied, gave full particulars of the cakes. This also resulted in some business.

This woman claims that baking Christmas cakes for small businesses can be very profitable. She says, "How hard and how many months you work depends on how much business you get. There is a steady demand, and year-round sales, if your product is top quality."

70

Planning Children's Parties

Many mothers frequently have to give parties for their children, or those of friends, but are lost as to how to go about it.

A person offering such a service might be surprised at the demand. When you think of it, a children's party can be both an interesting and exciting venture. You would have to arrange the food, if this was to be part of your duties, but there is the entertainment. You could have a clown, a magician, maybe a pony ride if it was summer and the event was held outside. You might arrange to give the guests funny hats, play various games, and offer prizes.

Many mothers are not able, or do not have the time, to arrange parties of this kind, and many would pay to have a professional children's party arranger look after all the details. This idea is being operated in many areas. You would have to let it be known that you are available, and make contact with any people you would expect to hire. Sometimes local amateur magicians are available at an affordable fee. Your charges would have to be worked out on a basis of costs, work, and time.

Along the same lines of course is the arranging of parties for adults. But this is a bigger operation, including music, more involved food dishes, liquor, entertainment, location, and other factors. So obviously the fee charged would be considerably higher than for the kiddies' parties, which could be more fun.

71

If You're Handy with Your Hands, Visit a Gift Boutique

*B*outiques of all kinds are becoming increasingly popular. Some deal in merchandise manufactured commercially, while others specialize in homemade products or stock such items along with manufactured products.

The owners of such shops, mostly women, welcome new ideas, and new twists on old products.

If you like sewing, crocheting, knitting, etc., it might be worth your while to spend some time around such shops getting ideas. It very often happens that one person turning out a certain item can only produce enough for a few stores. Thus the same items produced by someone else might find a ready sale in other areas.

It might even pay you to travel a little, and visit gift shops in hotels. Make sketches of items that appeal to you. Get permission to take photographs of displays and buy a few articles. You'll seldom, if ever, get a "no."

When you have designed or produced some items, take samples around to likely shops. Most will want to carry your goods on a consignment basis, and will pay you about 60 percent of the retail price after the goods are sold. Retailers will often give you tips on which type of merchandise is most saleable.

72

Someone Has to Be Santa Claus

I recently talked to a retired man who told me he makes a considerable amount of money being Santa Claus. Apparently Santas aren't only in demand at Christmas, but also at birthday and other parties where they not only get a laugh, but also hand out gifts.

My Santa said he is six feet tall and this helps, but you need not be fat—a little synthetic stuffing will do, although I understand that St. Nick is, on the average, getting thinner all the time.

You must have a good "Ho Ho," have a genial personality, and be able to answer all sorts of questions from both children and adults.

Santa wouldn't disclose the fee he gets, but did say it was very good.

For Christmas, he starts the first week of November and runs to the end of the year. He has shopping center contracts, evening dances where he shows up, children's parties, and other gala affairs.

He says he gets some jobs through employment offices where he is registered, others as a result of people mentioning his name, and still others as a result of phone calls he made. He telephoned the managers and personnel directors of companies, and asked, "Having an office party this year?" He then followed this up with a series of "Ho Hos" and "I'd be delighted to be your Santa."

Apparently it brings in business.

73

Gift-Wrapping Is Pleasant Home Service Work

Working people, particularly those of younger years, often find they are so busy they don't even have time to wrap holiday gifts. Others, while they may have the time, don't have the knack. This applies particularly to men. There are also cases of companies who require the wrapping of a large number of gifts. To recruit staff members for this is usually expensive and unsatisfactory.

If gift wrapping appeals to you, you could arm yourself with rolls of wrapping paper, ribbon, and tape, and let it be known that your services are available.

If you anticipate a large volume of business you would be wise to get your supplies from a wholesale paper merchant. These people are usually listed in the Yellow Pages of the telephone book.

Charges for wrapping gifts vary, depending upon the size. Prices can range from one to four dollars.

Put your business card in a store that offers a bulletin board service, and this should start the ball rolling.

74

Making a Fortune in the Mail Order Business

It's a dream shared by many people: sitting at a desk in a corner of your home and opening endless stacks of letters which contain checks, money orders, and cash. Retirees in particular like this dream because whatever the weather might be, or the season, you're not exposed to the elements.

I suppose there has been as much time, money and effort spent searching for the profitable item and the advertising media to sell it, as has been spent on trying to locate new oil wells.

Millions of dollars are spent every year by mail order advertisers. Some have a product or service which brings them a steady profit, and others are still searching for the answer. One advertising manager of a magazine, which carries eight or more pages of classified advertising, told me that a great deal of advertising comes from senior citizens.

Advertising directed to people who want to get into mail order often promises all sorts of profits. Some of these ads sell booklets on how to succeed in mail order. They tell how to write ad copy, how to choose products, which magazines to use, and how to produce flyers. Other booklets explain what kind of products sell best. Some advertisers explain how to make one's own products and sell them for huge profits. The advertiser sometimes sells the ingredients.

Mail order can be a great business if you can develop or find a program that works. Some people develop an idea that is profitable from the start, while others try different ideas for awhile and then drop out because they can't afford the expense of advertising. They are soon replaced in the classified advertising columns by other bright-eyed hopefuls.

Making a Fortune in the Mail Order Business 175

Many of those who fail are like the old miners panning for gold. Many quit just before the big bonanza is discovered. You can usually tell the successful mail order operators. Their ads appear month after month, sometimes year after year, in a variety of publications. When someone hits a big one, you can be sure that dozens of other people will start advertising the same deal. This will continue until sales slow down.

Age is No Deterrent in the Mail Order Business
There are many senior citizens who are doing well in the mail order business. One is Dr. Jack Thuna who has a course in herbology. The doctor is eighty-six and owns the Emerson College of Herbology at 77 St. Catherine Street East, in Montreal. Although he has poor vision (he uses a magnifying glass to read), he is able to do most of the lesson corrections for his correspondence course himself. He uses the enquiry method of advertising and sends out a folder. His advertising is run primarily in publications pertaining to herbalism. He is an expert on herbs and has been in the business for many years.

Booklets Are Preferred
Choosing a product that will sell is sometimes difficult. You don't want a product that is available in every 7-11 store. It should be unusual, fill a need, offer value, and hopefully be relatively inexpensive to pack and mail. Your product has to be highly profitable to take care of all your costs.

That is why information booklets are the most popular items with sellers of mail order products. They can be produced at a local print shop in small runs. If you don't wish to write the copy you can engage a writer on a 10 percent of sales basis. Check with an authors' group for prospects.

Many small part-time publishers advertise a booklet before it is printed. Then, if results are poor, they either return the money to the customers or have the few copies they need to fill the orders photo-copied.

Don't Overlook Vertical File Sales
If you produce a booklet be sure and send circulars to

libraries. Mention the table of contents, price, and any other information that would help librarians make a decision as to whether or not they want to buy it. Some libraries, such as the Toronto Public Library and the Chicago Public Library, buy for a number of other libraries in their areas.

A copy of the booklet should go to the Vertical File Index, the H.W. Wilson Co., 950 University Ave., Bronx, New York 10452. This company mails a monthly publication to a large number of libraries in the U.S. and Canada. This publication contains information on the latest vertical file publications. Most public libraries have a vertical file system, which is a series of containers about three feet long in which paper-covered booklets are filed. This vertical file, as it is called, is usually kept close to other, larger books on the same or similar subjects. Some firms, such as companies who want to publicize a certain service, a new type of product, etc. send booklets free of charge to libraries. Libraries order directly from the publisher and total sales of one hundred copies is not unusual.

What Is A Booklet?

There has been all manner of argument as to the difference between a book and a booklet. Some years ago, most books were hard cover. Today, many books are published in soft cover. Many libraries say that a publication exceeding forty pages is a book, and less than forty is a booklet. A publication of a dozen pages or so is categorized as a report.

The Big Mail Order Market

A U.S. book publisher has said that not more than 4 percent of the population ever enters a bookstore. Think of your friends, relatives, neighbors—how many do you know who ever visit bookstores and make purchases? Maybe not even 4 percent. No one knows how many people buy booklets by mail, but the total has to be large. Moreover, the titles sold by bookstores and other outlets do not offer subjects similar to those sold by mail.

This week I visited three bookstores looking for anything on money-making ideas, the mail order business, how to sell photos, and self-publishing. All are popular subjects. No doubt there are tens of thousands of people who would like to know something about the preceding subjects. But I might as well have been asking for a book on directions for getting to the moon, or how to build an atom bomb. The retailers or their staff generally shrugged. One girl, when I mentioned money-making ideas, brought out a book on buying stocks. Another had a title pertaining to newspaper publishing, but nothing on self-publishing. It's no wonder the little kitchen-table publisher is often doing well with his or her booklet.

So find something that people want. Maybe even your bookseller will give you some leads. And you too might make it big!

I suppose hundreds of mail order booklets have been written and sold on identical subjects, proving that repetition is no deterrent to success. If you have something to say and know how to say it, then do it! For a retiree who writes and has a booklet printed, it can mean the beginning of a new adventure.

Last year publishers in Canada and the U.S. rejected some 400,000 book manuscripts. Regardless of this, small publishers, many of them operating from home in their spare-time, sold millions of dollars worth of information on how-to books, poetry, novels with a local background, and historic works.

Keep away from hard cover books. The covers alone can add three or four dollars to the price of a book without giving you anything. You're better to stick to forty- to eighty-page booklets. Your printing cost will be under $1 a copy if you handle it right, and your sales will be better if you keep the retail price at between $4 and $7.

You can sell through classified ads in big circulation publications (they are cheaper per thousand readers). You may not sell a lot of poetry or novels this way, but you can certainly sell information booklets, i.e., "How to do something," "make something," or "accomplish something."

George Had a Great Idea, Almost...

Fortunes have been made in mail order, and fortunes have been lost. It's one business where you really have to know what you're doing. Even that's no guarantee you will make money at it. Now take the case of the man who had, or so he thought, a great mail order idea.

George W., who lives in Toronto, had retired from the food business. At sixty-seven, after spending much of his retired time just driving around, he decided to go into mail order.

He knew nothing about the business. He had seen an ad offering a pocket hand-warmer that was chemically heated. It was guaranteed to keep your hands warm when watching football games or when engaging in winter activities. It sold for $19.95 and wholesaled at $10 in lots of 100.

This chap bought a sample of the warmer, walked down Toronto's Yonge Street on a chilly November day and came home raving to his wife that his money problems had ended. He was soon seated at the dining room table, figuring out how many people go to football games. He came up with totals running into the millions. "We'll sell all fall and winter," he said, "and then take a cruise. But I don't suppose people would want them on a cruise ship."

It may take a trained mail order ad expert a couple of weeks to write a page of copy and decide which media to use, but, my friend George was no slouch. By the end of the day he'd bought 100 of the heaters and got the price down to $9 each (by long distance phone to New York) and had prepared an ad and sent it off to a couple of Canadian sports publications.

He figured that there would also be some orders from hockey fans, bird wachers, hikers, skaters, and so on. He could hardly contain his enthusiasm. The ads (one-half page) cost him $500 each. He had been thinking of *Playboy* until he discovered it would cost him about $75,000 for a one-time full-page ad in color.

It would be a month at least before his ads would be out and by then his hand-warmers would have arrived.

His wife wasn't quite as enthusiastic as he was. In fact, she told him not to expect her to sign any checks on their joint account. If he insisted on going ahead with this sort of nonsense he would have to do it with his own savings. I think every company should have a middle-aged housewife on their planning board when bringing out new products or working on new ad campaigns. They'd save millions!

George's certified check was posted when someone mentioned duties, sales taxes, etc. Then he realized he would have to pay these costs, and possibly raise the price of his product. Now he had to phone the company in New York to find out if the $19.95 price was on the product.

"Indeed it is," said the firm's sales manager. "Right across the box in big letters. It's such a bargain!"

Now the Toronto man had a real problem. The warmers would cost him about $12-14, not $9. Well, the volume sales would look after that.

There was a frantic month's work getting labels printed, arranging a post office box number, opening a business bank account, renting a typewriter, and buying a small adding machine to total the profits.

At last the magazines went out and almost immediately George became a regular visitor to the post office. At first he brought a briefcase to carry home the orders. He figured the magazines had a total of about 100,000 circulation, and the publishers claimed there was a pass-along readership (friends and relatives who would see the magazine) of at least three per copy. This meant 400,000 readers. George figured conservatively that even if he only got orders from one-half of one percent, that would total 2,000 orders. At $19.95 each he'd receive $40,000, and some people would also buy extra warmers as gifts.

If it had worked out that way, George would certainly have been walking on air. As it turned out, there were only five letters in the mail box, and it had taken a week for the first to arrive. He explained to his wife, Marge, that the mails were slow and people didn't always read a magazine the day it came.

He looked at the five letters in the box and wondered how Marge would react. Five times $19.95. That was about $100! Even if he received only five orders a day, that would be twenty-five a week! $500! He should have quit the food business years ago!

He opened the letters slowly. He pulled out the enclosure from the first one. It was a single sheet of paper. He tapped it gently in case the check had got caught in a fold. But no money! The letter was from a religious group that offered to send him a free booklet that would give him everlasting life if he would send them a dollar for postage and handling. He dropped it into the waste basket.

Letters two and three were chain letters. The next one was from a publisher selling classified ads. The circular said a copy of their paper would no doubt arrive shortly. George muttered that it already had, and he wasn't interested. The last letter was from a man out west who said he would try three heaters, if he could have them on consignment, to be paid for thirty days after he sold them.

After that George didn't bother to bring the briefcase to the post office. During the next thirty days he received a total of seven orders.

The magazine publishers told him the second ad usually pulls better than the first, but George told them he had no more money to spend.

It was then that he made his first smart move. Each publisher, being small and understanding, agreed to accept part payment for the ad in hand-warmers (at wholesale).

Then they began running ads, and eventually, over two years, George got rid of his stock.

Nothing Ever Changes ...

I came across a *Popular Mechanics* magazine classified section a little while back. I glanced at the classified advertising section under "Business Opportunities."

One of the little ads caught my attention. It read, "Beat the Depression! Make a fortune! Send twenty-five cents for this great idea!" I looked at the date of the magazine. June, 1933! It was a depression year all right. I noticed the ad was circled, and I recalled I had sent a quarter away for the idea.

The idea was simple enough. Gillette Razor Blades were a nickel each, and if you had a tough beard you got one shave out of one. Maybe it was planned obsolescence. Anyway, for a quarter I learned that if I took an empty glass, put a little water around the edge, and rubbed the blade on the inside of the glass, I could increase my shaves to ten for each blade!

This advertiser wasn't through with me yet. He wanted to give me real value for my mail order quarter. He said that I had his permission to run the same ad as he was running and I could keep any quarters that came in. Today, the operator would probably make a franchise deal out of it and want to take back a percentage of the gross.

I wonder if I was dealing with the originator of the idea, or number 149 down the line.

All of which proves that things don't change very much.

Diet and Cookbooks Are the Largest Sellers

Bookstores report that diet books and cookbooks outsell every other type of reading material. Cooking first came from the Orient and most of our recipes had their initial development there.

For economic reasons, food is geographical in nature. For example, people who live by the sea usually include fish in most of their recipes.

If food is your hobby and you have a large number of recipes which you prize, you might want to consider putting them in book form. Even though some of the recipes may have been printed previously, you might wish to introduce your own little wrinkle which would make them new.

A catchy title and an interesting introduction will help you "sell" your book to a publisher. To find out who publishes such books examine publishers' catalogues in your library or check the index card file under cookbooks.

In the event that you would rather publish the book yourself, this can often be very profitable, especially if you tie-in with an organization which wants to use it as a fund-raising medium.

A lady in Nova Scotia wrote a book on seafood recipes. A local church decided to use it as a fund-raising project for its work. It cost about a dollar a copy (paper cover) to print. Retail price is $3. The church gets a dollar and the author gets the same. People in the town and surrounding areas buy it as a gift and it has a wide sale. In fact, it has gone back to press about every three years.

When having the book printed, consider plastic binding. It costs about ten cents for material per book with labor extra. You may be able to borrow or rent such a machine and do the work yourself. The operation is extremely simple and one of the main advantages is that when opened the book lies flat.

You might be able to develop a nice little business producing cookbooks, historical works, and so on for various religious groups and associations. A good financial plan is to base the cost of the book at retail as follows: one-third for printing, one-third for the association for their work, and one-third profit for you as organizer.

What Type of Product Sells Best?

No one really knows the answer to this question. Even costly surveys don't always give us the answer. Millions of dollars were spent proving that the Edsel would sell. No research was done on Monopoly; it had no elaborate introduction. Yet Monopoly has made millions and the Edsel car went nowhere.

In mail order it's the same thing. Years ago a young man began selling watches by mail. He started off in his spare time and he had only a few dollars for advertising. Then he took in a partner. They've done very well under the name Sears, Roebuck!

Timothy Eaton started off in a small way too. He had a store on the east side of Yonge Street, Toronto. When he had to seek larger quarters, and asked his wife for her advice, she said, "Go west, young man!"

So he moved across the street.

There is an oversized bronze statue of Mr. Eaton on the ground floor of the Eaton complex. The founder's left boot shines like gold where eager passers-by have rubbed it for good luck.

If a poll were taken booklets would probably come way out in front as a popular item for mail order. Today people want knowledge, but they don't like big books. Some book publishers, when speaking of educational books, avoid the use of the word book. They instead refer to sets of instructions, information booklets, guides, and often (when selling by mail) break a 250-page book down into ten booklets. And the word "course" is sometimes hard to sell, instead, "These ten booklets will give you all the information you need, quickly, easily, effortlessly."

Hints for Producing Your Own Booklets

If you write a booklet, set the type yourself unless you have a brother-in-law in the typesetting business. All you do is buy or rent a typewriter with a black, easy-to-read face, preferably ten- or twelve-point letter size.

Take a standard letterhead sheet of paper and fold it in half. What do you have? Obviously two pages of paper with four sides. Now take ten letterhead-sized sheets and repeat the process and you have forty pages. If they were printed, with a cover of slightly heavier paper stock, you would have a booklet.

Your pages should be crisp, clean, and clear. If you have used a carbon ribbon your work should be beautiful. No matter if you have pasted patches over errors, they won't show in the finished job. Watch for pencil marks where you may have originally marked errors and erase them. It's usually better to number your pages in the center at the bottom of the page, and even on short pages keep the numbers the same distance from the bottom of the page. When your work is printed the page numbers should be in line, not with some numbers a half-inch from the bottom of the page and others two inches up.

You may have included your cover in the total of forty pages, and the only additional charge is three or four dollars for slightly heavier cover stock. Most publications are printed on what is commonly referred to as twenty-pound stock. This is sturdy and economical.

For your front cover lettering you are better to use a type commonly known as Letraset. This is professional and is rubbed on like writing over carbon paper. For five dollars or so, you can get sheets containing dozens of letters and figures. The type is available in various sizes and type faces. Artists use it regularly, so I suggest you try it for cover work and possibly for the inside headings. It looks better than having someone do the work freehand.

Copy centers which are springing up everywhere and are sometimes known as "supermarket printers" issue price lists. They seem to all run about the same insofar as printing costs. A recent price sheet I received, good through the winter of '82-'83, shows that 500 sheets printed back to back, each sheet carrying four pages of your digest-sized booklet would cost you around $25. So forty pages, broken down to ten letterhead-sized sheets would cost you $250 for 500 copies of your book. Check with two or three copy centers if you don't get the price you want in the first place. For small runs like five hundred, copy centers use paper masters. The cost to them for these is about twenty-five cents each. Your printer will have to machine-fold your pages, and this shouldn't cost more than five dollars.

Now you take everything home and collate (put it together) and staple it. You'll need a stapler with a V-shaped base on which the books are held while you press the machine arm. This is just an ordinary stapler set on the V-base. I paid $38 for mine new. You can also get long-arm staplers but these are more expensive and more difficult to handle. The V-shape stapler always puts the staples in the right place. If the printer does this work, he has to pay the help and overhead, and costs start to run away. You should have your booklets for sixty cents each at most (forty pages) providing the printer only does the printing, folding, and trimming. But you don't have to do all your booklet collating at one time; do fifty at a time as you need them.

So, if your costs are say sixty cents, sell the booklet for $4 to $5 a copy. On a sale of 500 your gross profit could be two thousand dollars. And have a second booklet ready so you can send customers a folder when they buy your first booklet. Include the circular with the order and it will cost you nothing to mail it. Your customers can be regular buyers of your work. And, of course, check postal rates. Book rate is reserved for libraries and publishers, and offers a good saving. Publishers usually include invoices with the book.

The Value of Many Titles

One mail order person operating out of Virginia, told me he has been twenty years in the business and deals only in books. His books, or booklets, are eight and one-half by eleven inches in size, and average sixty to eighty pages. He charges $8 to $10 a copy. Today, most mail order people figure that production costs shouldn't be more than 15 to 20 percent of the selling price.

This person always offers the prospect a choice of at least a dozen booklets or books. He specializes in business publications, accounting, advertising, and management. His argument is that if they don't like one, they'll like another, which is sound. He also offers a small booklet free with some titles. Buy one book and get a less expensive one free. This is good business. People love something for nothing. I recently paid $10 for one of his books on advertising. I didn't want it, but I did want the free booklet which contained a listing of daily newspapers.

Repeat Sales Are Important
An advertiser will offer customers the opportunity of subscribing regularly to his lists because the money in mail order is re-selling to the same customers continuously. It costs you nothing to get them. Just send them circulars or offer them regular service.

An Ontario man runs this classified ad: "Government Crown lands. Fifty dollars and up. $2." He must get business, because his ad appears regularly.

Those First Two Magic Words...
The first two or three words in a classified ad are extremely important. They can make or break your ad. Many people just run down the edge of an ad column so you need a stopper, like merchandise in a store window, to attract customers.

You must get to the point fast. You want to attract the right type of reader (those who are interested), and also try to save money by using as few words as possible. There are professional agencies who specialize in writing classified ads.

The old clichés such as "Save Money," "Prices Slashed," and so on are too general for a classified ad, although they might pull in a newspaper ad where you have dramatic artwork or photographs.

Words in a classified ad that paint a picture in the reader's mind are good. Let's look at one. "Clip newspaper items in your home for big profits!" This is a nine-word ad. Now, examine the ad. Even if you could save a couple of words it would be worth it, providing you don't take anything away from the ad. So, how about this? "Clip newspaper items at home! Big profits!" We've cut it down to seven words and it's stronger. If you wish you can use ellipses, or three or four question marks, or exclamation marks without charge. These things make your ad look a little bigger without adding expense.

At the end of your ad you would provide details and address. There is no need to write a long ad when you are offering free information.

Then, when people write in, you would send them your folder which would tell all about your booklet which gives full information on how the reader could make money clipping newspaper items. You might have a twenty-eight page booklet that could sell for five dollars. A reader could get his money back by sending out just one clipping.

The Right Words Attract the Right People

Magazines such as *Mechanix Illustrated* carry many columns of classified ads. They have 100 or more column headings that you can choose from. The circulars they send out, as do most other publishers when requested, mention these categories. If you were selling a booklet on clipping newspaper items, you might choose from such headings as "Income Opportunities," "Home Money-making Ideas," "Business Opportunities," "Hobbies," and others. You might find yourself among twenty-five other advertisers, all offering opportunities, but it's not likely they would have the same product as you.

The so-called attention-getting action words in advertising are: new, different, guaranteed, free, proven, sample, easy, secret, amazing, as well as a few others.

Experienced classified advertisers advise the entrepreneurs not to give the reader a choice, such as "two for $3 or five for $7." The readers likely become confused and won't buy at all.

How to Key Your Ads

If you place ads in a number of publications and the returns start coming in, you'll want to know which magazines are pulling, and how well. This is accomplished by placing an identifying figure or letter beside your address number. Let us say your street number is 100. If you were advertising in the *Vancouver Province*, your address might appear as 100-P. A Chicago paper might be identified with the letter C. If an ad were running in January your address might be 100-V1. There is no charge for this service, yet it can give you a complete check on the publications you are using.

Some firms using display ads where there is no individual charge per word use more elaborate keys, such as "Write desk 15, Dept. 15" or "Write Mr. Smith, or Jones" and so on, each name corresponding to the name of a publication and other data to the advertiser.

Fast Returns from Dailies

When you place an ad in a daily (I found Sunday editions best), you get your returns by Wednesday. They'll come in at least until the following Monday.

In the big weekly tabloids, which come out Mondays or Tuesdays, you'll start getting returns in seven weeks. Although these tabloids, with their millions of circulation, come out early in the week, they are purchased primarily on Fridays and Saturdays. This is because they are popular sellers in supermarkets, and weekends are the principal shopping days and women are the big buyers. I understand that seniors make up a large percentage of their readership. So, if you develop a booklet for retirees, it could pay you to consider the tabloid market.

Rates in tabloids average from $3 to $5 a word. It takes about twenty words to tell a convincing ad story. One advertiser told me he uses the words "Satisfaction Guaranteed."

Consider Magazine Time Lag

Monthly magazines normally need copy six to eight weeks in advance of publication. A week after magazines reach the stands you'll receive your first mail. These letters will probably be chain letters and solicitations from various publications seeking your business.

One executive told me that his publication of two million circulation figures that 10 percent of readers read their three classified pages. So this gives you 200,000 prospects.

188 Making a Fortune in the Mail Order Business

There are fantastic stories of returns from small ads. My biggest return on a booklet was from one radio interview, and I received over two hundred letters containing almost a thousand dollars. And the publicity was free!

The Ideal Mail Order Proposition

The ideal mail order operation is one where you can advertise an item for cash. Two to five dollars is a popular price. From the classified ad you get enough returns to pay for the ad, pay for whatever material (product) you send out, pay for any printing, and the postage. At the same time you include another offer, and this offer makes you the big profit. You usually can't make any money by selling to a customer only once, so you should have something additional to sell. Your biggest cost is going to be your advertising to get that customer, so you must capitalize on it. How much business would Sears do if they only sold to a customer once?

Said one mail order dealer, "I sell books and booklets. Every two or three months I send out a folder to the same people, plus, of course, to some new names. I have been selling to old customers for three years. I don't keep a big stock of books on hand. I go through the classified sections of *Popular Science* and *Popular Mechanics* and under 'Books and Periodicals' I can get some very good booklets for resale."

The Excitement Makes It Interesting

Mail order is like Blackjack. You never know what card you are going to draw.

Once I ran a classified ad that cost me $25. It pulled poorly. I may have broken even. Then two months after the ad appeared, a chap in Los Angeles bought a copy of my dollar (wholesale price) booklet on writing. He apparently liked it because shortly after I got a money order for $200 with a note: "Please rush this order. I can't keep up with the demand!" How he sold my booklets, or where, I never found out. I suspect he started his own publishing company after the initial success he had with my publication.

Some people in mail order, particularly those starting out, often experiment. One couple sent me a large check in payment for some cookbooks they wanted. When I explained that I wasn't in this line and that I was returning their check, they sent it back and asked me to send them whatever I was selling. Their note said, "If you are honest enough to return our check, your products must be good and we want to sell them." It turned out that this couple was buying booklets, and holding house parties at which they gave little talks on these booklets. I hadn't thought of this angle before. I guess almost any type of product can be sold at house parties. Such parties are held to sell food, cosmetics, clothes, jewelry, cooking utensils and other products, so why not books?

The Ad That Keeps Pulling

If you get a little classified that offers a real service, it's like having a bank account with unlimited funds.

I heard of a chap who has been running the same ad for months and months. It's only about twelve words including the address. The ad reads, "Government surplus. Lists of bargains, $2!" He pays $5 a word for his ad or about $60. He uses the mechanics-type publications and gets approximately one and a half million audited circulation per magazine, or four million readers (most magazines claim three to four readers per copy). Multiply this by three magazines a month (about $200 costs) and you have a circulation of eighteen million. Obviously they don't all see his ad—if they did he could retire forever. But enough readers respond with $2 to make his little business venture profitable. I believe he gets his "Surplus" information from government handouts, and he weeds out the best. He offers a monthly newsletter service, and a lot of his customers buy this. A circular is included with the customer's original order.

Mail order offers a challenge. My only advice is don't spend more money than you can afford to lose, because no matter how you check it out, it's still a gamble.

75

How to Use Free Publicity to Promote Your Business

*I*f you start a little business, don't forget that publicity can help you promote it. Radio, TV, newspapers, and magazines are always interested in people who accomplish something, or are trying to. And when it comes to people living in the area of the media's circulation, you have an even better chance of getting publicity. This is not saying you can't get publicity elsewhere too. If you promote your business properly you can be a one-man publicity band that can draw a lot of business. Try for an approach that is unique or unusual. This will make you newsworthy.

The Model Boat Man
   Herb Slack of Ottawa, retired, started devoting his time to a hobby he had long loved—building replicas of famous old-time ships. Sir Francis Drake's *Golden Hind* is one of his best known creations. Other ships, such as scale-model copies of yachts, are in demand too. He gets $100 to $700 a model and sometimes more. But this craftsman in wood will also make you a birdhouse to order if you wish.
   He tells a fascinating story about the ships he builds. He sometimes gets blueprints from the government of 15th-century sailing vessels. You can tell he knows his business and media like CBC love to have him on the air. The publicity helps Herb's business too.

The Woman From Washington
   Skippy Muir of Haliburton, Ont., formerly of Washington, D.C., bought a small log home in the Laurentian Mountains which she visited while on holiday.
   She became annoyed when she couldn't find any infor-

mation about modernizing her home, adding running water, electricity, and insulation. So she and her husband started a magazine, the *Log Home Guide*. Her husband was on the verge of retiring and now has a new interest in life.

The magazine was started in the late seventies, and is now sold across the U.S. and Canada.

Skippy credits a great deal of her success to the free publicity she obtained from the media. This included some of the country's largest magazines and newspapers, such as *The New York Times* and its syndicate.

So whatever you are doing, think publicity.

76

Should You Join the Credit Card Services?

Depending on what kind of business you are in will usually determine whether or not you should join one or more of the credit card services.

When I was active in the mail order business, I joined Visa. I found this to be a simple matter. A young lady calls at your place of business, fills out a form which you sign, you get a merchant's number, and that's it. The cost to join used to be $25; that's a couple of years ago, so the fee is probably higher. If you require the little machine in which your customer's card is inserted, and registered on the bill, there is a small annual rental charge, which also includes maintenance. Of course, because I was doing business by mail there was no way a customer was going to mail me his or her card along with the order. So in mail order you bypass this step. In lieu of this card you do the following when an order comes in by mail:

You write or rubber stamp (which is better) your name and address on the printed form which the bank gives you at no charge. They will charge you a percentage fee for giving you immediately the amount of money shown on the form. To identify you as a member of that credit card firm, you will jot down your merchant's number. You will also include the name and address of the customer, and general product bought, such as "books." You must include customer's card expiry date and the customer's card number.

If the order is over a certain amount, $15 with Visa, you must phone a certain number and get authorization. That's to make sure the customer is good for the amount. If you get the okay, that means the bank guarantees the amount. However, your job is not finished yet. If the amount is under

192

$15 you are supposed to check a long list of numbers which you will get weekly. This list is so long you may wonder if there are any good customers left. While all of this sounds a little complicated, you will get a form explaining everything. You get a verification number to call for each credit card member bank; even if the customer lives 5,000 miles away you get an almost instant report.

The percentage you are charged for this service varies depending on how much business you do per month with the card company. I was paying 5 percent of the total amount which was deducted monthly from my account.

Merchants report that the main advantage of taking credit cards is that people spend more than if they were paying cash. In mail order it has the effect of letting the customer buy without having to get a money order, make out a check, or send cash. It extends a note of confidence to the seller which is always a valuable asset in mail order. You are also protected which is not the case with checks. You will find that about 10 percent of your business will be through credit cards.

77

Some Tips on Where to Get Information

*E*veryone starting a small business requires information; it might only be an address, or background on a product or service.

A letterhead is valuable when requesting a free booklet, samples of magazines, advertising rates, etc. In fact, their use can almost become a hobby in itself.

Just have your name and address typed at the top of a standard-sized sheet of paper. Use or obtain the use of a typewriter with a black ribbon. A carbon ribbon is best.

Take the sheet to a copy center. They will print from your copy. Their work is quite inexpensive and these centers are springing up all over. If possible, mention on the letterhead the type of business you are in or intend to be in.

One Source to Avoid when Seeking Information

It's usually a waste of time to write to magazines or newspapers for information. These people are a hard-working group who have no time to even read requests for information, let alone answer them.

When I was publishing, in the midst of a bag of mail containing manuscripts, ads, contracts, checks and subscriptions, there would be a letter or two like these:

"I have to prepare a thesis on the lives of animals. I have chosen the wolf. It would be appreciated if you could send me answers to the following questions: main habitat, are they a source of food, is it legal to trap them."

And, "I enjoy your farm magazine. I want to do a book on pigs. This is where you come in. Could you please send me a history as to how pigs came to this country. Is it true that

many were sent from Ireland during the potato shortage? If
I could have this information in ten days it would be appreciated."

Was I supposed to take someone off a magazine for a day
to do research for a reader?

General Sources of Information

There are five standard sources of information, apart from
reference books, which I use regularly, and if one can't supply
the information, one of the others usually can. The sources
are: the Chamber of Commerce in the city or town in which
you desire information; the Board of Trade; the city, state or
provincial publicity department; the central public library;
and the Bell Telephone company. Some Bell offices either
maintain or have information regarding Bell yellow pages.

Reference Thoughts Worth Filing

In the event that you consider selling books, don't overlook
Chicago. It is considered to be the remainder (publishers'
overstocks) capital of the world. If you can't get hold of a
Chicago telephone book (yellow pages) which lists dozens
of wholesale book sellers, contact the Chicago Board of Trade,
141 W. Jackson Blvd., Chicago, Il., 60604.

Additional Free Services

If you have difficulty locating numbers in the phone book,
you are probably aware that all, or most, Bell offices will
make no charge for operator assistance calls if you secure
a letter to the effect that you have reduced eyesight. You
can get such a letter from your eye doctor. This can be
forwarded to your Bell office for their approval which is
usually given.

Another free service is direct dialing for information on
long distance numbers. Normally in the U.S. or Canada, it is
just necessary to dial 1, then the area code of that city,
followed by 555-1212. Then you will get an operator who will
get you the number desired. If this is a company it is often
not necessary to have the address, and if you don't have it,
the operator will often give it to you.

A 240-Page Helpful Book from Ottawa

"Assistance to Business in Canada" is loaded with information that will be helpful to anyone contemplating starting a small business, and it may be had by writing to: Assistance to Business in Canada, Ministry of State for Economic Development, Ottawa K1A 1E7.

The CASB (Canadian Assistance to Small Business) program will be of interest to senior citizens in particular. This is a management counselling service in which retired business people act as counsellors to assist owners and managers. This service is designed to help small businesses, and executives are paid by the government for their expertise. If you are knowledgeable in a certain phase of business and have some spare time, why not contact the government? There is a nominal daily charge to business for each counsellor assigned. For further information on this program, contact CASB at the address given above.

The U.S. Government, Washington, D.C. has produced a series of small booklets, under the general heading of "Business Starters." They are available by contacting the SBA, Small Business Administration, National Technical Information Center, Room 620, 425-13th St. N.W., Washington, D.C.

The Superintendent of Documents publishes a weekly checklist of documents available covering such subjects as business, economics, science, and the environment. This weekly report is available from the Government Printing Office, Washington, D.C., 20402.

You Can Volunteer for Overseas Government Work

Both retirees and those who have not reached retirement may apply for specialized executive work outside of Canada. This is a federal division, the name of which is Canadian Executive Service Overseas. The head office is located at 1130 Sherbrooke St. W., Suite 350, Montreal, Quebec, H3A 2M8.

CESO is interested in people with all types of skills: farming, journalism, mechanics, lumbering, building, and scores of others. People are sent to South America, India, and the Caribbean, and many other parts of the world. This is primarily instruction work and each assignment lasts from three weeks to several months. While this is volunteer work, all travel expenses are paid, and there is a daily living allowance. When I talked to CESO they said that they have over one hundred people overseas now and are always anxious to get applications. If they can't place you immediately, your application is filed for later consideration.

Universities, Colleges and Governments Offer Opportunities to Retirees

Did you know that some colleges and universities are now offering special summer courses that can help you make money, and even have a new career?

One-week courses, which include room and board, are now available from a number of universities and colleges. Some charge $150 a week "all found."

Dozens of subjects such as pottery and art are taught by professional teachers. The courses are only available during the summer vacation period after the students have left. But you'll have to hurry to register.

A friend tried to register at one Maritime college in February, and was told they were all booked up. So it might be wise to write to two or three institutions, to be sure of securing space in one. You could ask for their brochure showing subjects, as these often vary from college to college.

Continuing Education

While not all colleges or universities offer live-in accommodation for seniors, a great many do have continuing education facilities.

There are often a wide range of studies, frequently given at night, and some offer material which would be an aid to earning a second income.

These courses are often available throughout the year, and a telephone call or letter to the college or university of your choice should bring you a descriptive folder.

Your Library Can Make You Rich!

We all live off ideas, just as we live off each other. If you're going to be successful you need ideas, and probably the best place to find ideas is in your library. Just about every idea you can think of is hidden away somewhere in those thousands of tomes which are a mystery to many people.

The cross-index system is well worth examining. If you know only the author's name you can probably find the titles he wrote, or if you know the title but not the author you can find the answer in the card system. But probably of more interest to an ambitious person like you is the opportunity of finding books about subjects you know little or nothing about. Just ask your librarian to show you the subject cards. You'll find leather craft, sheep-breeding, book-binding, and endless other topics which could open a new life to you.

One of the most important sections in a library is the reference department. This is where the directories, some costing as much as $100, are kept. Fortunately, most libraries have copying machines, because reference books cannot be removed.

More Money-Making Ideas for Retirees

78

Florida's Plant Doctor

*H*ere's a great idea for people who know all about plants and flowers. There seems to be more great ideas coming out of Florida than any other state or province. I suppose the climate attracts the seniors, the good weather makes them feel ambitious, and presto! another idea is born.

The Plant Doctor operates around the Clearwater area. A lot of people have gardens but don't know what to do when the baby geranium gets sick. Well, down there they call the Plant Doctor. He also has a weekly column in the local paper.

If you're an expert on horticulture you might consider this business. I suppose you could be on-call like the regular doctors used to be. Your fee could be based on a "per call" basis, or on a monthly service charge like the fellow who cuts the lawn.

This sounds like a fascinating business. The length of the growing season would depend on where you live, but remember that many people have house plants that require care and attention too!

79

A Coffee Route Works Anywhere

I met Mr. Adams at a party in a small town on the Ottawa River. As I recall, his entire conversation was filled with excitement about a small business he had started two years earlier. "It's so profitable," he said, "that I want you to promise you won't use my name or town. If you do, I'll be overrun with competition."

But he did explain his business to me. After 20 years with an insurance company he quit to go on his own.

Mr. Adams had noticed over the years that various companies were provided with coffee services of various kinds. Most were machines in which you dropped a coin and drew your coffee from a spout. Two other spouts were present, one for cream and one for hot water. People used hot water to make soup or tea.

Mr. Adams decided he could invent a better system. He went to a wholesale coffee machine company and looked over their units. He found that for $50 he could buy an aluminum coffee maker. He also found out that while the large coffee machine companies went to the larger offices, factories and so on, the smaller outlets, because of their small needs, were often neglected. So he set up in a small town and used that as a base from which he called on nearby small towns. Keep away from the cities, he said.

He would call on a prospect with his Silex or Silex-type coffee maker and sell the company one or two machines at retail. He bought a half-dozen at first to earn the wholesale rate. Mr. Adams would explain to the prospect that his machine could be plugged in anywhere. (No special electrical costs.) Each month he would deliver packages of powdered cream, sugar, coffee, stirrers and napkins. The cost would run $40 to $100 a month depending on quantities.

A card would explain the simple coffee making directions, and the company would appoint one person for one or two weeks to make the coffee. Mr. Adams, who is getting on to retirement age, told me that he signed up 23 customers in the first couple of months. The main reason companies want the service is that it prevents staff running off to the nearest restaurant for coffee. Secondly, he guarantees everything, and will be there for service on a regular basis, or when he is needed.

He uses his car; there is nothing heavy to transport and the whole operation is going well.

In parting he said, "Your mind is like a muscle. You have to use it regularly to get the most out of it."

80

A Fix-it Business through Retailers

Most retailers, especially those in small towns with only one or two staff, aren't experts in the repair of articles such as toasters, irons, blow dryers and so on.

About five years ago, E.J. started a small business repairing such items in Montreal's west end. I learned about his business through a hardware store in my neighborhood; in fact, E.J. fixed my toaster.

When I talked to him early in the year, E.J. said he had 53 customers spread over a 25-mile area. He calls on his customers once a week; hardware stores, small grocers, gift stores and anyone else who wants to offer a repair service.

The repairs for my toaster cost $14.50, and when I pointed out that that was what the toaster initially cost 15 years ago and complained about the high cost of repair, the hardware man pointed out that my toaster now cost $50. Of the $14.50, the dealer gets 40 percent and the price is set by the repair man who does most of the work himself. So, it is a good deal for both the repair man and the dealer.

E.J. is close to 60 and is not worrying at all about his age. He figures that down the road he can always hire people to do the repairs as he continues to call on the trade.

81

Managing an Apartment Is Great for Retirees

I met a man who had worked for Air Canada until he retired. He lived in Vancouver and was looking for something to do, so he ran a classified ad saying he would manage an apartment building for the owner. He got two calls and took over a 60-unit building.

He has a list of people who specialize in repair work for buildings. If something goes wrong he calls in one of them and then sends the bill to the owner.

This manager also collects the rent. He has a friend in the building who takes over when he goes on vacation.

In return he gets an apartment and about $200 a month. If it's some little thing he may fix it himself, but most repairs are done by outside help.

This gentleman claims that a deal like this is ideal for retirees.

82

Mr. Ukon Is a Most Unusual Handyman!

Mr. Ukon lives in Japan. For many years he had been steadily employed by an electric company. And, like many people, he had often thought of giving up his job and going into business for himself. He wasn't a well-to-do man, but made a comfortable living. But about three years ago he did quit his job, and put an ad in the newspaper: the heading read, "Handyman Available!" But there was one difference. He said he was willing to do anything — anything legal, that is. His friends who had called him in when the sink was plugged would continue to call him, except that our handyman would now charge for the service. He is quoted as saying that there are all kinds of sophisticated machines around, but none that will repair or fix the little things right away.

His business is a success and was from the beginning. Women call him in to fix light bulbs they can't reach, they ask him to go to the supermarket for groceries, walk the dog, or sit with an aging aunt. He has regular customers who call upon him. Mr. Ukon, in a translated radio talk, said that his work has opened up a whole new life.

And did the business grow? You bet. He now has 50 employees and a dozen apprentices who work for free in order to learn the business. He has at least three girls answering the phones, and he's only sorry he didn't start out before. He doesn't worry too much about such specialized work as plumbing and electrical jobs; he says there's enough small work for him to make a good living. Maybe there's something there for an ambitious senior over here?

83

Don't Neglect the "New" Brain Pool

Some startling facts come from one business executive who said, in the *Saturday Evening Post*, that one person in nine today is 65 or older, but in the next half century this figure will rise to one in six.

Another speaker points out that there is a vast pool of knowledge and experience in our seniors that we can't afford to overlook. This will become more evident in the next 20 years because of the decline in the number of our youths by 16 percent (in the age bracket of 18 to 24).

Said one executive who employs senior citizens, "Many seniors have acquired a skill over the years that makes them very valuable and a part-time job gives them the opportunity of putting these skills to work. Putting them to work creates a sense of usefulness and 'belonging' that is missing in their lives, particularly those who live alone."

84

Hartford Insurance Firm Introduces Unique Job-Bank Program for Retirees

*I*t was in 1981 that the head office of the Travelers Insurance Companies of Hartford, Connecticut, introduced their job-bank plan. Simply, this is a temporary employment program for retired company employees. At the time of the introduction of the plan only four or five firms in North America were using a similar, less elaborate plan. Now in full operation, the program can be used as is, or with modification, by just about any company anywhere.

The job-bank for retired Travelers employees is operated by a division known as Personnel Administration. Said a company spokesman, "We have many needs throughout the year for temporary help. These needs result from workers' illnesses, vacations, time-off needs and workload peaks. These various positions demand a variety of skills. Prior to the adoption of this retirement program, spare-time help was supplied by employment agencies. It was realized, however, that former employees have many plusses. They have a knowledge of the company, its operating methods and the location of most, if not all, of the departments, such as the cafeteria, etc."

The bulk of assignments are of a clerical nature. At times special skills are required which may call for former staff members who served in an executive capacity. Positions are hourly paid and on the average last two to three weeks, but occasionally longer. Retired employees are invited to phone or visit the personnel department if they are interested in registering.

The company reports that since the plan was introduced, the results have been very impressive. Those who apply may work part-time or full-time at temporary employment. On some jobs, which require a full day, job sharing has been introduced.

Back in 1981 a Travelers spokesman said, "We regard ourselves as a Christopher Columbus in this field and I doubt if there are more than three or four companies with a similar plan." Reported Robert W. Feagres, Senior Vice-President of Personnel Administration, "Flexibility underlies the company's program."

In the years ahead, companies will find that the labor pools are shrinking, says Travelers. Experienced people are often hard to get. The result is that more and more firms will have to turn to older workers. A survey conducted by the insurance company showed that 85 percent of retired employees of 65 and over would be interested in some form of paid employment. The majority said they preferred part-time work. Some 41 percent were so enthusiastic over the idea that they said they would consider early retirement if part-time work was available.

During the first ten days that the plan was announced, there were 120 enquiries for information.

Workers report that they enjoy going back to work and meeting old friends again. Employees often return to their old departments. Pension or security plans are not affected by the additional income. Many employees said it wasn't so much that they needed the money, but it gave them something to do. A retired employee might be called back a number of times during the year. Many employees had retired three years before going back. They told of all types of things they were doing to keep active — traveling, needlepoint, attending lectures and so on. But it was often expressed that retirees felt that they needed something that would keep them on a schedule. Said one retiree, "The job gave me a challenge, stimulation and excitement." One woman who had retired after 44 years is now back, after a year of retirement.

Evelyn M. Smith, Co-Director, Senior Job-Bank, told the author, "The job bank started March 16, 1981. Within a short time 136 retirees were enrolled in the plan, but we could use many more. Of the 136 enrolled, many have volunteered to continue working on a part-time basis. They handle such jobs as mail processing, filing, advanced computational work, van driving, rewriting job descriptions, special projects and secretarial duties. During the work vacation period, we could use many more typists and secretaries. This is our weakest link."